SELF-MENTORING™:

THE INVISIBLE LEADER

By

Dr. Marsha L. Carr

Self-mentoring is trademarked by the author (2011).

Visit the website at:
www.selfmentoring.net

Table of Contents

Foreword

Mentoring is as old as the hills and there are many versions of mentoring – it takes many forms. The subject of this book is a particularly intriguing variation of the core model of mentoring.

Some years ago, I was delivering a mentoring skills workshop and one of the participants said, "I think you kind of mentor yourself really!" Well, this book is all about that idea! It offers an interesting and easily developed model of mentoring to unlock an individual's potential.

I am a mentoring person. I am an academic and a practitioner. I have received awards for my contributions to mentoring. In my opinion, this book breaks some new ground and adds to the literature in mentoring. The notion of 'self-mentoring' can be viewed as either a development of the core model or a part of it. This foreword is driven by three questions:
1. What then is the core model of mentoring?
2. Where does it come from?
3. How does it relate to self-mentoring?

The core model and where it comes from
The earliest, and most often quoted version of mentoring is found in Homer's ancient Greek poem, *The Odyssey*. Close analysis of the old text reveals that the original mentor was not particularly good at his job (reminiscent of Dr. Carr's experience of mentoring!) and had to be replaced by Athena, the Goddess of wisdom and warfare. The successful mentor was a Goddess in disguise! That makes it a tough act to follow for lesser mortals!

Most of the story is spent preparing Telemachus, King Odysseus' son, for a big battle. This battle comes at the end and is particularly violent, bloody, and full of vengeance. It is curious that so many people who write about mentoring omit this part and focus only on the developmental journey of the young prince Telemachus!

5

However, it is possible to glean something of the core mentoring purpose we might recognise today. It is a story, in part at least, about education, development, and leadership. Some of the core tensions we find in today's world are highlighted in *The Odyssey*. For example, the preservation of the state through the leadership development of the young prince could be a parallel for modern day tensions between the organisation's (the state's) needs and those of the individual. These elements are often in tension as Dr. Carr highlights in her example in the early part of this book. Organizational politics and how to steer your way through them! Telemachus and Odysseus ultimately did it with vengeful violence! In the modern world, we must do it peacefully, shouldn't we?

The old story is also a model of experiential learning, with Athena offering experiences to the young prince, from which she knew he would learn. Both of these elements relate to modern mentoring discourse and fit with self-mentoring.

Much time passes!

Some writers link mentoring to medieval times (Darwin, 2000; Murray, 2001), particularly through traditional guild-type apprenticeships and knight/squire relationships. However, accounts of the period show that these relationships were not called 'mentoring.' Although they were often one to one, they could be exploitative and manipulative. The master craftsman would use the apprentice as a source of cheap labour with the promise of progression in the chosen trade. However, the craftsman often would not behave honourably. He might pass the apprentices' work off as his own or keep the apprentice under tight controls by restricting food and payment. This type of behaviour was clearly exploitative and a misuse of power. Whilst these elements are not considered part of modern mentoring, there is evidence that such behaviours could still exist in theory and could be a source of some modern day negative perceptions of modern mentoring. This is discussed a little later.

In eighteenth century Europe there were five publications about mentoring:

1. Fénélon's (1651 - 1715) *Les Aventures de Télémaque* (1808) – an educational treatise
2. Louis Antonine de Caraccioli's (1723-1803) *Veritable le Mentor ou l'education de la noblesse* (1759) translated into English in 1760 to become *The true mentor, or, an essay on the education of young people in fashion*
3. Honoria (1793 and 1796) published three volumes of *The Female Mentor*.

Both Caraccioli and Honoria based their writing on Fénélon. These volumes provide an experiential model of education involving reflective questions and challenging learner centeredness. They articulate the importance of learning relationships, trust, listening skills, and good questioning skills. Arguably, this was the start of mentoring, as we know it today and not the Ancient Greek version, which is so often misquoted as being the source. However, not all modern mentors receive this kind of development as mentors. Whilst many claim to be 'flattered' to be asked, they may not have any of skills appropriate to mentor. Some become mentors by virtue of their experience and the risk is that they just might share that by handing out irrelevant advice. Self-mentoring helps to avoid this problem.

Levinson et al (1979) presented another version of mentoring in the book *The Seasons of a Man's Life*. The term 'mentor' was used to describe someone, often half a generation older, who helped accelerate the development of another in his age related transitions (the book was about male development). Levinson et al (1979) develop a framework of age related development based on age transition. They link this to Jung's (1958) psychological concept of individuation. Levinson et al (1979) suggest that mentoring could reduce these age transitions from an average of seven to three years for those with mentors. This very quickly became the catalyst for a rapid growth of mentoring for accelerated career progression in the US. The logic was simple, get a mentor and you'll get on faster! A deeply flawed and naïve logic!

In *Passages: Predictable Crises of Adult Life* (1976), Gail Sheehy discusses adult development mainly from the female perspective. At that time, she noted that mentoring relationships were not common among women, however some 20 years later, in her revised edition, *New Passages: Mapping your life across time* (1996) she adds developmental maps on both male and female development and notes that mentoring had become more common among women.

Still in the US, Kathy Kram produced much good quality research on mentoring. Her main contribution is the idea that mentoring performs a *'psychosocial function'* (1983:616). The theory is that the mentee is socialised into a social context and develops self-insight and psychological wellbeing. Socialisation is a key issue in this book.

Zaleznik (1997) suggests that *'psychological biographies of gifted people repeatedly demonstrate the important part a mentor plays in developing an individual.'* He argues that leadership ability is developed through these intense and often intuitive relationships which have the affect of *'encouraging the emotional relationship leaders need if they are to survive'* (p.78). Emotional maturity and leadership development are key themes in this book.

Berman & West (2008:744) argue that mentoring increases *'accurate awareness about one's emotional intelligence skills'* and many writers (Clawson, 1996; Mullen, 1994; Zey, 1984; Levinson et al 1978) link a mentor's unconscious motivation to Erikson's (1978) psychological concept of 'generativity'. To be generative is to be proactive in making an impression on the world, to be productive and constructive. This is another theme in this book, but mentoring one's self draws on one's own resourcefulness and confidence rather than accessing them with the help of another person.

Mcauley (2003) employs the psychological concepts of transference and countertransference in order to provide deeper insight into the power dynamics that may be at play between mentor and mentee relationships and it is here that many of the difficulties with 'traditional mentoring' sit and underpin Dr. Carr's experiences of mentoring. Power differentials create disempowering messages. Self-mentoring, employing Dr. Carr's process, avoids this problem.

Clutterbuck and Lane (2004) outline two main models of mentoring - the US *'career sponsorship'* model and the European *'developmental'* model, although there is evidence (Kram & Chandler, 2005) that mentoring in the US is changing to include a more developmental approach.

The *'sponsorship'* model creates a problem for the more traditional mentoring models in that it is focussed on accelerating progression. This brings with it many advantages for mentee, mentor, and their host organization. Carden, (1990) and Allen et al (2004) note that on the positive side, the sponsorship mentoring activity can enhance knowledge, emotional stability, problem solving, decision-making, creativity, opportunity, leadership abilities in individuals, and organizational morale and productivity. However, in contrast, Ragins, (1989 & 1994); Carden, (1990); Ragins & Cotton, (1991); Ragins & Scandura (1999) all show that a career sponsorship orientation can be exclusive and divisive, encourage conformity among those with power, maintain the status quo, and reproduce exploitative hierarchical structures. These elements can also lead to the relationship breaking down or becoming abusive. Again, this is also evidenced in Dr. Carr's direct experience.

Some studies (Clutterbuck & Lane, 2004; Garvey, 1995 Rix & Gold, 2000) show that *'developmental'* mentoring offers the same kind of positive benefits as identified within the US model but with fewer negative effects.

Other more recent models of mentoring attempt to negate the power elements. This may be achieved my considering the education and development a mentor may receive before becoming a mentor. It may also be achieved by considering carefully how 'the organizational scheme' is designed and how participants are briefed in its application. Peer mentoring and reverse mentoring are also new additions to the mentoring model. These are aimed at reducing power differentials in order to create a more open dialogue, which is not distorted by power

So, open dialogue focused on development is key, but power distorts - enter self-mentoring!

This book provides powerful and practical insight into the self-mentoring model developed by Dr. Carr. The process is clearly articulated and rooted in the key principles of experiential learning, reflection, and reflexivity. Without these elements there can be no development or progress. Added to this, Dr. Carr is inviting people to value their own resourcefulness, to pay attention to their inner positive voices, and act on them. Self-mentoring is an empowering model of mentoring. Bring it on!

Professor Bob Garvey
York St John Business School
York
UK

Acknowledgments

I personally want to thank the following people who, without their guidance, this book would never have been possible…

Jennings Lambert, my husband, for always being supportive and a stronghold in high winds.

Dr. Robert 'Bob' Garvey, my dear colleague, for his insight and wisdom.

Avil Beckford, for being my 'Invisible Mentor'.

Susan Finley, for the countless lunches to get me on track and help me commit.

Angela Housand, for always being there.

Fran Scarlett, for your guidance and expertise in business.

Ron Vetter, for believing in me.

Bethany Tap, for those incredible video production skills and long hours of production.

Graham Elmore, for getting self-mentoring in Wikipedia.

Kevin Derajtys, for reading everything ever written about self-mentoring and actually enjoying it.

Bethany Meighen, for all your positive energy.

Lisa Hunt, for all the therapy sessions.

Domonique Adrian Dixon, for your incredible skill at webpage and app development.

A special thanks to the University of North Carolina Wilmington's *Center for Innovation and Entrepreneurship* (CIE) for guiding my entrepreneur spirit and supporting my business venture.

Introduction

I am a survivor. I survived my first year in a new profession, a new position, and what I perceived as a hostile environment. I not only survived it, but I was successful in finding my passion while meeting my expectations. I look back now and realize that those early months during my first year were more instrumental in my success than I ever anticipated. How often, as a society, do we monitor the daily operations during the first several months of an incoming president in office? These are the impressionable months where opinions are developed and scrutiny surfaces. I was not a stranger to public inspection.

After serving for 30 years in public and private education, the last decade as a school superintendent, I was ready for a change. During this ten-year administrative span, I served under the direction of nine different boards of education, and developed a strong central office administrative team. As the first female superintendent hired in the county, I worked a minimum of 80-hours per week, which included many public engagements that absorbed my weekends. *I lived for my job.* There was literally no time for anything outside of this routine.

As my contract came to a close, I was ready for a new role that included a decrease in work hours and less politics, something more time-manageable with added rewards and incentives. After reading a Forbes Magazine 2014 Internet poll rating a college professor as the least stressful employment position in the US, I decided upon higher education.

I packed up and moved three states away from my former residence to a warmer climate and a new culture. I swapped the North for the South. It was exhilarating. Happy to find a sanctuary from the public eye as an administrator, I wanted obscurity in my new environment. I wanted to be inconspicuous – I was going to be an *invisible leader.*

I was so ready for this new adventure that I cast aside all my years of leadership experience and saw my future only in a positive light, neglecting to recognize the imposing dark clouds that loomed in the distance. Upon my arrival, I was greeted with smiles and warm welcomes and quickly assigned a mentor. My mentor, by all standards, was exceptional as a decorated sage with an expert track record in publishing, speaking, teaching, and research. He was funny and personable. I absolutely treasured him. However, despite my mentor's exceptional qualifications and my past leadership experiences, there was a chasm that could not be bridged over time. As talented as my mentor was, he had been in higher education his entire career and I came from a different world, one that practically spoke a different language. The challenge felt insurmountable at times. Within just months of my hiring, the department chair vacated the position and for the remainder of the academic year, our department fell under the guidance of the dean who, while extremely capable and competent, was already overwhelmed with duties. And to compound the situation, I recognized shortly after my arrival that two existing factions within our small department were in silent war. One faction hired me. This angered the other faction, who then, before my arrival, attempted to thwart my final employment. As each barrier was revealed, I wanted to become less and less visible in reaction to the turmoil of my surroundings. I was no longer in a friendly environment and I was terrified, not knowing in whom I could trust. I was suddenly alone in a foreign land. I was reminded of the scene in the movie, *Titantic*, when Leonardo DiCaprio was holding onto the floating headboard that kept Kate Winslet adrift and safe from the freezing waters but would inevitably contribute to his death. I was his character, Jack Dawson, and my demise was imminent. To have any chance of survival, I would have to find my own headboard if I were to persevere.

Assessing my skills as a leader, I called upon my strengths. *What skills would benefit me the most and what were the impediments?* I did what I knew best – I organized. I looked beyond my oppressing walls and called upon my prior experiences to formalize a plan.

In the first semester after my arrival, I had to create two courses from scratch using an online platform of which I had no familiarity. Terrified to reach out to anyone but my mentor, whom I learned didn't teach online and was without the means to provide assistance, I called upon university services and attended trainings during the year to ensure that I was a stronger online developer and facilitator in future courses. To battle my inadequacies in research, I reached out to others in the field that were successful and shared my passion. I spent the year establishing an external network and resource chain to help me navigate within this new environment that was very different than I anticipated and quite foreign to my leadership training. I spent as many hours reflecting on my writing and direction as I did in the company of others who provided different perspectives and shared their wisdom.

One of my early encounters was with a veteran professor from a neighboring university who was amenable to professional conversations. Within one year, I co-authored a book under his guidance. I soon realized that I had the skills to maneuver within my environment and manage my own personal development. Still, other weaknesses surfaced. I was without departmental support, so networking opportunities with local administrators and other necessary supports that were provided to other colleagues were not available to me. I had to create my own opportunities – no one was going to hand me anything. And so self-mentoring evolved like a phoenix from the ashes of despair.

Self-mentoring grew from a seed of necessity – my passion to succeed. My first presentation on self-mentoring was so well received that I began presenting and sharing my journey with others who were piqued with curiosity. I realized I was not alone. There were countless individuals with similar stories who felt that self-mentoring could be the headboard that Jack Dawson needed for survival.

Individuals, attending my presentations, wanted to know how they could learn to self-mentor. At the time, I didn't know the answer, but I was willing to explore the possibilities. I conducted a pilot study in a local, interested school district. This first study focused on a small group of volunteer teachers. The group spent a year learning about self-mentoring and implementing it under my tutelage. In turn, I was permitted to collect data, analyze the results and determine if self-mentoring was an efficacious practice. The results of the study were startling, even to me (Chapter 8) and suggested that self-mentoring increased confidence and augmented self-efficacy among teachers in and out of the classroom. There were other influences but these remunerations were more individualized and could not be identified as established patterns without additional support. I celebrated. But I needed more evidence, so additional studies began immediately.

This book opens with an overview of self-mentoring in Chapter 1. Chapter 2 will provide the evolution and placement of self-mentoring among such time-honored practices of mentoring and coaching. Chapter

3 introduces the process of self-mentoring to include the four levels that will be more detailed in Chapters 4-7. Chapter 8 will summarize studies conducted over several years with a wide array of participants including preK-12 teachers and university faculty, as well as outline future studies planned with administrators and students. Chapter 9 will share the impact and benefits of applying self-mentoring to everyday life in any profession as evidenced by self-mentors in the field.

I hope that you will see the value in self-mentoring and accept responsibility for your own personal and professional growth. The reward is self-confidence as a leader and courage to reach even what seem to be the most unattainable goals. After all, you are your own best mentor and it is *"Your Life; You Lead."*

SECTION I

THE ART OF SELF-MENTORING™

1

The Practice of Self-Mentoring

> "It is our duty as human beings to proceed as though the limits of our capabilities do not exist."
>
> *-Teilhard de Chardin*

First Day – New Environment

You arrive at your new job. It is your first day. It is so exciting to be starting a new position. You arrive a little early only to find a parking space within feet of the entrance designated as yours with your name embossed on a metal sign. Impressed, you park and get out of your vehicle. As you begin to walk toward the building, you notice the entrance way is designed in an ultramodern, contemporary style with manicured lawns and colors that burst from the landscape. Your mood heightens with each step. You dressed professionally in order to look your best. Before you can reach the eight-foot tall glass doors, a greeter meets you. He offers you a glass of orange juice (freshly-squeezed) and some tropical fruit choices (probably fresh as well) from a tray. You smile, graciously accept the flute of juice and walk with your new friend. As you enter the opulent building, a couple more 'new' friends are awaiting your arrival. Two are standing by the doorway and introduce each other as your personal assistants. One takes your coat as well as your empty flute. The other one offers you a gold-embossed, scripted itinerary of your day. Your orange juice is now replaced by a Starbucks coffee – Venti-Soy-Latte -which is, surprisingly, your favorite. Your assistants smile as one leisurely commandeers you down a brightly lit corridor with skylights and exquisite abstracts adorning both sides of the walls. As you admire the sumptuous artwork, you are aware of little traffic during your hallway trek. When you do encounter another person, they stop to shake your hand and welcome you by name. You arrive at a tall, oak-trimmed, etched glass door that already has your name inscribed on it as your assistant motions you to enter. Inside you find a massive room that boasts a private bath, the latest in technology, a personalized mobile phone with all the emergency numbers programed, and an iPad equipped with meeting agendas and notes for your day.

If this was your experience when you started a new position, then you are in paradise and need to be thankful. This book is intended for those not in this world. Most of us do not have the luxury of such inviting environments, but we all must believe this type of environment exists.

For those of you that have a slightly different view of the first day, let's see if this is closer to reality. Let's reverse this scene and have you enter again.

You pull into the driveway looking for signs that direct you to parking. With little guidance, you find an area and hope that you have found an appropriate parking spot, from which you will not be towed minutes after departing or which you will discover to be the vice-president's ten-year-old favorite parking spot. You are like a new student on the first day of school, full of apprehension and desire. It is exciting yet you are also filled with anxiety as you wonder if you will like the job or if it will meet your needs.

As you enter the building, you are greeted by the buzz of workers, all of whom are strangers to you. You make your way to what appears to be a reception area or kiosk and wait for someone to notice you. Eventually a man approaches you and asks if he can help. Once you identify yourself as a new employee, you are greeted with a smile and a handshake. The man yells at one of the people contributing to the perpetual buzz, motioning her to come forward. You are handed over to this colleague who greets you with another smile and hastily ushers you down a dimly lit hallway. You weave in and out of passersby with little acknowledgement from them until you stop abruptly in front of a door that you are told is yours. And just as you arrived, you are now alone again. We won't even bother describing the room inside. You already know what it looks like and what it contains.

While these scenarios are at opposite ends of the spectrum, most of our experiences will fall somewhere in the middle of these extremes. First day perceptions and feelings, by all account, are representational of the climate of the organization and set the tone for your success or failure, if you do not take charge.

Think of yourself as a detective investigating the organization by searching for clues that tell a story. You want to know everything about this new organization in order to solve the mystery of how you will be able to function successfully in this environment. What you may not realize is that your success is dependent upon your ability to do this. You must take control and seize every opportunity to gain knowledge of your environment, the individuals surrounding you, and how you can fit into this environment to be successful. You have the ability to be a leader in your life and write the script. You begin by *self-mentoring*.

Self-Mentoring

What is Self-Mentoring? Self-mentoring *is an individual of any age, profession, gender, race, or ability – YOU – willing to initiate and accept responsibility for self-development by devoting time to navigate within the culture of the environment in order to make the most of the opportunity to strengthen competencies needed to enhance job performance and career progression.* So what does that mean?

Within each of us, sometimes hiding from the day-to-day drama, there is a leader – often invisible –another side of us that can rise to the occasion, a side that knows what to do during a crisis or when challenged. We often call this our inner voice or leading with our heart, but the truth is, we are following our intuition and the innate, instinctive path of a leader.

The urge to lead is stronger for some than others. When these instinctive yet hidden skills are not called upon or used, like a car door never opened, they become rusty over time. Exercising these skills is like putting oil on a rusty door hinge. The more you open the door, the better it functions and practice perfects these skills. Your skills will become more ostensible as you apply them to situations. However, if your skills are dormant, think of them like a sleeping volcano that can suddenly rise up to the occasion. The most obvious examples are in moments of chaos.

In the summer of 2006, several sections of New York City became the victim of an unresolved series of power outages resulting in what is often referred to as the 2006 Queens Blackout. It was during this blackout that a friend of mine was caught in traffic on her way home from work. She described ordinary citizens of New York getting out of their vehicles and directing traffic, helping others to remain calm, and providing directions to walkers who abandoned vehicles in an attempt to get to shelter. In the midst of chaos, people, who may never have taken any leadership initiative prior to this event, calmly used their leadership skills to provide assistance and bring comfort into the lives of others. It is this internal voice and sometimes dormant self that will be solicited and cultivated when necessary or under extreme conditions. The next several chapters will provide you with a more detailed overview of how we begin the process of self-mentoring and find the leader within.

Unleashing The Leader Within

As a self-mentor, you must either already know yourself or get to know your talents and avoidances as well as factors that positively and negatively impact your engagement with and within the environment. You must already be or learn to be confident in who you are and who you want to become. Self-mentoring is as much about the person you are in the present as it is about being able to project into the future to see the person that you aspire to be.

To really know yourself, you must be honest. Sometimes it is easier to be honest with others than to be honest with ourselves. We often lie to ourselves; we tell ourselves things are fine to stimulate a calming effect, even when we know deep down that this is not true. We tell ourselves the present circumstances are acceptable and don't need to change, but intuitively we know this is not an accurate assessment of the situation. Self-mentoring encourages you to be honest and learn how to critique yourself in a manner that promotes self-development. It takes courage to take these steps, but self-mentoring is as easy as deciding that you are going to accept responsibility and commit to your own growth without the presence of another individual to nudge or motivate you.

Self-mentoring is a journey of discovery that you progress through in four levels. The levels—*Self-Awareness, Self-Development, Self-Reflection, and Self-Monitoring*—are detailed in Chapter 3. You complete one level before proceeding to the next. You determine the pace and progression through each level. There is not a stopwatch or high score. You remain at each level as long as you need in order to feel accomplished. To begin, there are three areas of concentration: *1) your environment, 2) those in your environment, and 3) YOU*, as shown in the following chart.

Table 1.1

Environment	Shared Space	YOU
How you interact with the new or existing environment	How you interact with those in your new or existing environment	How you see yourself interacting with others in this environment

The Environment

Self-mentoring is the art of leading oneself in an unknown or even hostile environment, like the uncomfortable work relations I faced as a new faculty member. The environments in which you interact, whether at work or in other capacities related to your career, are not always transparent. The hurdles I faced were concealed during my initial interview visits. These hidden barriers and political layers shrink or block your ability to succeed unless identified. Self-mentors develop strategies to overcome these barriers and acquire tactics to approach precarious conditions.

Think of your organization as a living, breathing, and ever-changing complex system of interlocked subcultures (Schein, 1992) defined by a set or network of interdependent components that work together to accomplish the goals of that organization (Lezotte & McKee, 2002). Within this complex system, there are multiple layers that you must be able to identify or recognize as they relate to you. You must identify implied and often un-implied meanings.

A culture that respects differences in opinions and supports learning has been embedded in the ethos of self-mentoring. A culture that is ripe for debate and dialog to test the boundaries of prior practices and thinking fosters the practice of self-mentoring. A culture that discourages differences and punishes learning can be challenging for even the most experienced; however, as a self-mentor, you develop strategies that make it possible to overcome.

The culture of any organization speaks loudly, but you must get beyond the top layer that is most visible or most obvious upon first inspection. You must penetrate the other layers, often concealed, for a more realistic assessment. If you have ever bought cantaloupe, you know that you use your senses to select a perfect fruit. You feel the cantaloupe for soft spots, scan the surface for discoloration, and 'smack' the loupe for the right sound that implies ripeness. Still, regardless of all your effort to purchase the best cantaloupe by external assessment, you are only inspecting the surface. You will not know what is under the tough, protective hide until it is cut open and you take the first bite. You might have selected a loupe from which every bite is succulent and sweet or it may be hard and bitter.

A self-mentor learns to be their own quality-assurance team by inspecting the environment and asking questions such as, *Is this an organization that respects and values employees and are employees viewed as a central component to the success of the system? Does the organization have a strict by-the-book work ethic or are rules changed accordingly for individual situations? Is it an encouraging and relaxing work environment or is it threatening? Are incentives built in to motivate you or is everyone treated the same, regardless of productivity?* Not only must you know your environment, but you must also become equally familiar with those with whom you interact and share the environment.

Shared Space

You share your work environment with others, the personal struggles, work ethics, successes, failures, and the very air that you breathe. You may work at a desk, in an office, or consistently in a team. Regardless of your position, you often interact daily with those in your environment. Through these interactions, you can uncover valuable information. You will meet individuals that are resources and those that you can befriend. You will detect groups of power that can be assistive and groups that can be disparaging. The information you gather about those in your environment is just as critical in understanding yourself and how you either fit in or don't as it is to the steps necessary to find a niche or create a safe harbor. Some questions to ask are:

- *Are your coworkers happy at work?*
- *Do they enjoy work related interactions?*
- *Do you fit in?*
- *Is this a place you love to work?*

- *What are accepted and unaccepted behaviors?*
- *Are you comfortable with the conversations?*
- *Are your coworkers respectful of each other and the leadership?*
- *Is there a culture of respect?*

YOU

You are a living, breathing organism that has unlimited and unparalleled potential because you can think. You have the ability to experiment and explore your potential, yielding limitless success. Self-mentoring provides the flexibility to achieve at your own pace, on your schedule, and for the duration you want in order to thrive.

According to Linda Lambert (2003), a scholar in the field of leadership development, leadership is a process, not an innate or taught set of individual skills. She believes that leadership includes problem solving; broad-based, skillful participation; conversations and stories among colleagues; and task enactment in the environment. Those who aspire to become leaders and understand the necessary commitment need encouragement and a structured approach to reach their full leadership potential. Self-mentoring provides this.

As we close this chapter, let's find out about your confidence as a leader. On a 1-10 scale with 10 as the most confident; rate your confidence as a leader. There is not a right answer. If you believe it to be true, then it represents your perceived confidence as a leader.

| 1 | 2 | 3 | 4 | 5 | 6 | 7 | 8 | 9 | 10 |

You will be asked to complete the same exercise in the final chapter for a comparison of how you view yourself as a leader before and after self-mentoring. Now that you have a better understanding of self-mentoring, let's move on to the next chapter and read about self-mentoring in relationship to two invaluable practices: coaching and mentoring.

Chapter Summary

When you arrive at a new position or new profession, there is excitement as well as ambiguity. You may embrace this experience or you may feel anxiety. Regardless of your personality, you do have the ability to make this transition smooth and effortless. You will learn to call upon your hidden or dormant leadership skills and develop a plan for your success as you practice self-mentoring in your environment.

Self and Peer-Reflection Activities

- *Try to describe self-mentoring to a colleague or friend. Anticipate questions they may have so that you can respond.*
- *Reflect on how you would use self-mentoring in your present setting.*
- *Think of a past position you held and how self-mentoring would have benefited you.*

2

The Evolution of Self-Mentoring

"Whether you think that you can or
you can't, you're usually right."

- Henry Ford

Across the Atlantic Ocean in the United Kingdom, Dr. Robert Garvey, a business professor at York St. John School of Business, has examined historical references to search for the origin of two practices – coaching and mentoring. In terms of mentoring, Garvey shared that there are several different beginnings of mentoring as identified in the Foreword. Coaching, he concluded, also has a presence in early history. Regardless of the ancestral roots of these two practices, Garvey and I both agree that they have a strong presence today in business and education.

Mentoring and coaching are often used interchangeably in conversations (Garvey, Stokes, and Megginson, 2008). And beyond that, there are the numerous meanings assigned to each practice in any given situation. Mentoring and coaching have become nationwide emphases in both education and business in the United

States as research increasingly suggests that professionals benefit from the guidance and service of a mentor or coach (Allen, Eby, O'Brien, & Lentz, 2008). And now another practice, self-mentoring, has yielded positive results from preliminary studies in leadership development.

This prompted my need to travel to York to meet Garvey and introduce self-mentoring to colleagues as well as the business community in northern UK. Garvey, editor of a six-volume series entitled the *Fundamentals of Coaching and Mentoring* (2014), is an expert in the field of mentoring and coaching. He has spent a lifetime studying and learning about mentoring and coaching, so it was only natural that I would seek out his expert opinion in determining the relationship between self-mentoring to coaching and mentoring.

Self-mentoring is moving to the forefront of current support and leadership practices and gaining national attention as a complementary practice or viable alternative to individual or group mentoring and coaching programs (Bond & Hargreaves, 2014, Carr, 2011; Carr, 2012).

Coaching, mentoring, and self-mentoring each have parallel yet exclusive characteristics that inherently brands each practice or combination of these practices. When selecting a practice, consideration should be given to the specific needs of the individual or the organization as it aligns with each practice. An overlap of the three practices is exhibited in Illustration 1.1.

Illustration 1.1 Coaching, Mentoring, and Self-Mentoring

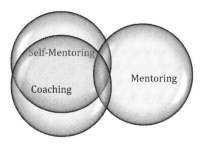

There is a noticeably stronger relationship between coaching and self-mentoring in comparison to mentoring. Both of these practices, coaching and self-mentoring, shift the power to the individual. This is not as prevalent in the mentoring practice, where the mentor is viewed as guiding the individual or the mentee's progress. Self-mentoring, like coaching, accentuates tenets of individualism, autonomy, choice, self-leadership, and self-belief. Central to these practices is the idea of self-development (Huang & Lynch, 1995). Each practice advocates for the personal and/or professional development of an individual.

Coaching

Coaching is a process that guides an individual or group of individuals for the purposes of improving personal or job-related performance. The basic tenant, individuals have the answers or they can find the answers (Whitworth, Kimsey-House, & Sandahl, 1998). This has not changed over the years. Coaching continues to focus on what the individual (the coachee) wants whether it is to achieve a personal transformation or a performance goal (Garvey, Stokes, &

Megginson, 2014). In most coaching situations, the coachee controls the meetings and dictates the pace as well as the agenda (Whitworth, et. al).

Schools are indecisive on the practice of coaching. Most educational coaches offer an array of instructional support in literacy, math, and reading where the focus is often on classroom instruction. There are advocates for student-focused coaching, especially in early reading programs (Hasbrouck, 2007), but it is not presently a common practice.

Businesses use coaching as a technique for guiding individuals in their own personal and professional development. It can be argued coaching plays a different role in education than it does in business. School coaching programs are more akin to business mentoring practices. This alludes to our previous finding that coaching and mentoring are used interchangeably and defined by the user.

Mentoring

Mentoring is a common acclimation practice for individuals (mentees), who may be new to an environment or a profession (Schoenfeld & Magnan, 2004; Nakamura & Shernoff, 2009; Alred & Garvey 2010). The practice involves two or more individuals working together collaboratively to provide support and guidance to the less experienced or lower ranking of the individuals. It can be considered a partnership, in which both derive benefits from the exchange (Thomas & Saslow, 2011). Mentoring programs, for the most part, are designed to support the mentee for the first several years of employment and, in the most fortunate of cases, can subsist a lifetime.

As a new employee, you are assigned a mentor – someone to support and guide you successfully in this foreign place. This mentor will be selected through a variety of processes that range from a formally trained mentor to a simple volunteer. In the best of scenarios, your mentor will be selected from a wide array of potential candidates that are matched to you by race, age, gender, profession, or goal similarities as well as strengths/weaknesses to compliment each other. In the worst of situations, the mentor is the only person who agrees to 'take you on' after being badgered or threatened by superiors.

Let's assume you have been assigned a mentor and a meeting is scheduled for you to meet this colleague. It unfolds as follows:

Your mentor is a veteran employee that has worked at the organization for over 20 years and is soon planning to retire. She is friendly and her personality is inviting. After a brief introduction, you begin to ask her questions about some procedure or policy. After a smile, your mentor explains that the organization doesn't strictly embrace following procedures or policy by the book and it is not a necessity to become familiar with it. Problems are solved using a 'common sense' approach and you will learn it over time. A similar reply follows each of your areas of inquiry. As you close the meeting, she suggests you write her a note and leave it in her mailbox if you have any questions. You smile back as a courtesy, contemplating how you are going to get support for your instructional needs.

When the pairing of a mentor and a mentee is compatible, a relationship of trust is built; however, when the mentor and mentee are mismatched, the results are often disastrous and referred to as 'negative mentoring' (Allen, Eby, O'Brien, & Lentz, 2008; Burk & Eby, 2010). There are five types of negative mentoring practice experiences: general dysfunctionality, mismatch within the dyad, lack of mentor experience, manipulative behavior, and distancing behavior (Allen, et al, 2008; Burk & Eby, 2010). General dysfunctionality is caused by the interference of a mentee's personal problem, a negative attitude to the work environment or to individuals in the setting, or a general lack of responsibility. Dyad mismatch is when both the mentor and mentee report a mismatch in personality type or work ethic. Lack of mentor expertise occurs when the mentee believes the mentor lacks the necessary skills – interpersonal or knowledge-driven - to serve as mentor. Manipulative behavior exists when the mentoring position is used for power, influence, or politics. The final type of negative mentoring is distancing behavior, which results when the mentor intentionally neglects to provide the mentee with proper guidance or sufficient time (Allen, et al, 2008).

Despite these negative mentoring examples, mentoring programs remain indispensable in providing new faculty or employees with essential support. The power of mentoring is in the opportunity for collaboration, goal achievement, and problem solving that it so often provides when successful (Ragins & Scandura, 1997; Nakamura & Shernoff, 2009; Thomas & Saslow, 2011).

Finding the Right Fit

There are times when coaching or mentoring may not satisfy your needs or the needs of your organization. Self-mentoring complements coaching and mentoring practices and provides an alternate route to having a coach or mentor. It is the practice of learning how to be your own coach or mentor. Since the goal of most organizations is to strengthen internal leadership, self-mentoring is a natural path. *Why is self-mentoring a natural path? Why would you choose to self-mentor? What can you expect to gain from the experience?*

Commitment

Driving the efforts of a self-mentor is commitment. Without commitment, you cannot fulfill your self-mentoring obligations. You must be willing to commit energy, time, and an open mind to the process. Self-mentors personally commit to their continual growth over the years in the absence of a formalized structure. This is key for the sustainability of what is learned from the process. Self-mentors are responsible for their own achievements. Whether this means changing behaviors or adapting new skills, they are personally dedicated to achieving their goals and maintaining behavioral changes. Oakes, Quartz, Ryan, and Lipton (1999) believe that, unless there is a commitment from those involved, the prevailing unwanted behaviors return. Self-mentors are viewed as more committed and passionate about sustaining their success because their sense of accomplishment is so motivational that it yields personal empowerment and a sense of self-efficacy.

Self-Efficacy and Confidence

Self-efficacy, a term that refers to how confident an individual feels about handling particular tasks, challenges, and contexts, is derived from Albert Bandura's social cognitive theory and is basically your judgment of your own capability. Converging evidence from controlled experimental and field studies verifies that belief in one's own capabilities contributes uniquely to motivation and action (Bandura, 1997; Bandura and Locke, 2003). As your perceived capability or self-efficacy increases, so does your confidence in your leadership abilities. The need to amplify your self-efficacy occupies a pivotal role in contributing to your motivation and in your accomplishment of your self-mentoring expectations. As a self-mentor, you become more confident as you recognize that you possess the skills necessary for navigating any setting. You now see yourself as capable and competent.

You become more comfortable with your ability to problem-solve and feel empowered to alter what is not working or change what is necessary. As your confidence increases, so does your self-efficacy. The cycle continues. A stronger, more confident leader emerges.

While leading one of my first self-mentoring training sessions, a teacher in one of the school districts, who was new to self-mentoring, shared her fear of speaking before a group. It is not uncommon for teachers to speak before students all day and then to harbor great anxiety when speaking in front of their peers. In my experience, I have found that many teachers are introverts. Therefore, while this was not shocking, the severity of her anxiety was alarming. When it was suggested to her that she use a video camera to film herself and then watch the footage with a trusted friend in order to get comfortable with speaking, she adamantly refused. She finally agreed to do a video snapshot – approximately one to two minutes in length - over a period of time to watch privately. Eventually, she increased the amount of time she videotaped herself in her classroom. She observed teachers in other classrooms and watched videotapes of her peers. After months and months of effort, she gained sufficient confidence in her ability to teach and now believed that she had something meaningful and valuable to share with others.

In my personal endeavors, I was confident as a leader from years of administrative service; however, my new environment was annihilating my self-efficacy. I doubted my capability in this new system, but my ability as a leader served to function as a strength and as pivotal in my success. These are only two examples of how self-mentoring can increase confidence and self-efficacy. Additional stories are shared in Chapter 9.

Chapter Summary

In this chapter, you learned how self-mentoring is woven into the complexities of mentoring and coaching. Each practice provides viable support for individuals in new positions or new careers. The key is learning how to use each of the practices when needed, in order to be successful in your environment.

Self and Peer-Reflection Activities

- *Try to describe self-mentoring, coaching, and mentoring to a friend.*
- *Reflect on your present environment. Which of the three practices is most beneficial to you presently?*
- *Try to envision a time when you could have used each of the three practices to help you succeed.*

SECTION II

THE ACT OF SELF-MENTORING™

3

The Levels of Self-Mentoring

"If I have the belief that I can do it,
I shall surely acquire the capacity to do it
even if I may not have it at the beginning."

-   *Mahatma Gandhi*

If you ever enrolled in a Karate or even Judo class, you know there are levels of advancement based on your performance. Your attainment at one level determines your advancement to the next. Each level builds on the skills you learned from the previous; you became proficient one step at a time. You are self-motivated to reach each level and, as your skill level improves, so does your confidence. These levels of these programs, Karate or Judo, are akin to self-mentoring, since the practice requires you to be self-motivated in order to reach each level of skill development. It becomes your personal goal to achieve.

In intermediate elementary classrooms across the US during the late 1960s and early 1970s, fourth- through sixth-grade teachers were encouraged to use the SRA (Scholastic Reading Achievement) center. The SRA center was a large, rectangular box that sat on a table in the classroom where students visited after completing their homework assignment. The box was filled with brightly colored six-by-eight-inch cards representing different reading comprehension levels, arranged by difficulty. The colored cards contained a story and the reader would shade in the correct responses for each story. Completing eighty percent of the questions correctly for each story in a level advanced the student to the next level. A large chart posted in the classroom showcased each student's success. Students were motivated to try to get to the next level more quickly than their peers. Those of you not born prior to the Information Age can think of it as a hard-copy electronic game. Students could only advance once they achieved a certain level of skill development, so it took self-motivation to aspire to reach the top level. The more you read, the more your fluency and comprehension improved as well as your confidence and self-efficacy as a reader.

Self-mentoring is a four-level, tiered process. While there is not a test at the end of each level or a wall chart to motivate you, you complete each level to advance to the next. The four levels are: *Self-Awareness; Self-Development; Self-Reflection; and Self-Monitoring* as seen in Figure 1.1. Each level applies the skills learned in the previous level. This illustration depicts the process as a staircase that you climb. However, the actual practice of self-mentoring is cyclical and more similar to Figure 1.2.

Figure 1.1: The Levels in Self-mentoring.

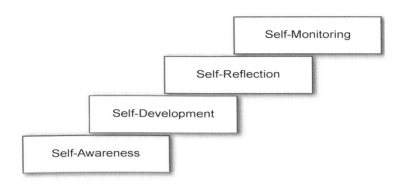

Figure 1.2: The Process of Self-mentoring.

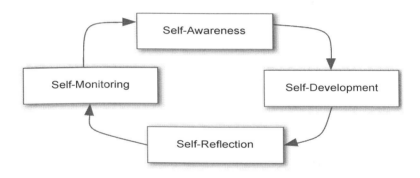

Completing each level is an individualized process akin to Judo advancement or SRA progress. The factors that determine your progress are dependent upon your personal motivation, time devotion, practice, dedication, and development of a viable plan.

A more detailed overview of the process through each of the levels can be seen as a flow chart in Figure 1.3 on the following page. This chart depicts all four levels as a continuous process.

Figure 1.3: Self-mentoring

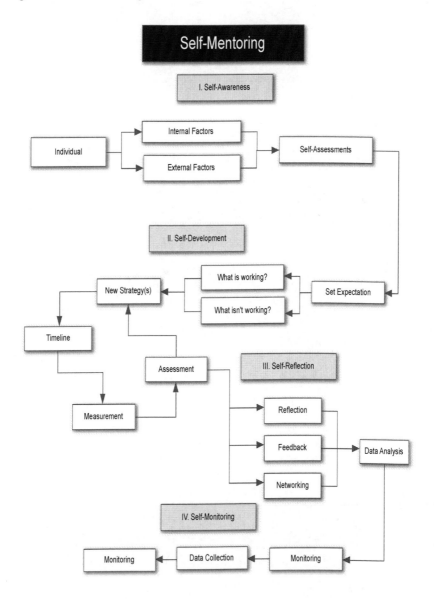

You begin at the first level in self-mentoring: *Self-Awareness*. This level is designed to provide foundational skills that you will use throughout the other three levels. A closer examination of Level 1 can be viewed in Figure 1.4.

Figure 1.4: Level 1- Self-Awareness

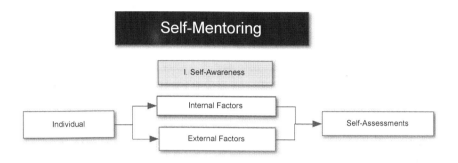

During self-awareness, the focus is on YOU and your environment. You become knowledgeable of both. Using self-mentoring activities and self-assessments, you capture the culture of your organization. You collect information about those you work with in the organization. Finally, you look in the mirror and identify your talents and your avoidances as a leader. Using collected information, or what we refer to as data, you isolate the skills that you have and determine what skills are necessary to succeed in your organization. Comparing your talents and the skills necessary to succeed in your organization, you determine what strengths you use and what strengths you need to cultivate. Once this level is mastered, you proceed to the next level, *Self-Development*, as in Figure 1.5.

Figure 1.5: Level 2 - Self-Development

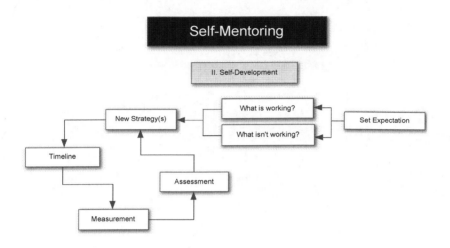

During the self-development level, you begin formulating a self-mentoring plan. You list all of the expectations that you have. The expectations can be related to your work in the organization or they can be behaviors that you want to change. You then select one expectation on which you will directly focus.

The expectation you select drives the strategies and measurements you will use to capture and assemble data. It will also determine the development of the timeline for your data collection process. It is important to provide sufficient time so that you will have meaningful data. Because your timeline for collecting data is dependent upon your expectation and strategy, the length of time to complete this level will vary. Once your plan is finalized, you move to the next level in self-mentoring, *Self-Reflection* as shown in Figure 1.6.

Figure 1.6: Level 3: Self-Reflection

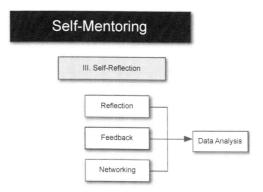

During the self-reflection level, you analyze and reflect on the information you have collected during the implementation of your self-mentoring plan. You can self-reflect or you can use a colleague or friend to provide feedback for peer-reflection. You learn how to use this information to alter your behaviors, change patterns, or increase your ability to succeed in your environment. Reflecting on the process and the data is critical at this level of self-mentoring. You may decide to collect more data and repeat the process or, if you have sufficient information, then you can advance to the fourth level, *Self-Monitoring*, shown in Figure 1.7.

Figure 1.7: Level 4 - Self-Monitoring

During the final level, self-monitoring, you determine if and to what degree you have achieved your expectation. If you are not satisfied with your status, then you may choose to collect more information until you feel you have successfully met your expectation. Once you are satisfied with your success, you need to determine how to monitor your status. In some cases, you may find that you met the expectation through the development of the practice or skill as a habit. If you have altered your practice or developed a new habit, you can repeat the process with another expectation. If the practice is not a habit, you may choose to develop a monitoring plan (Chapter 7).

Self-Mentoring - *If It Were Steps*

For those of you that need a more concrete image of how to self-mentor, ten steps have been aligned for each of the four levels as seen in the following chart.

LEVELS	STEPS			
Level 1: Self-Awareness	Step 1	Step 2		
Level 2: Self-Development	Step 3	Step 4	Step 5	Step 6
Level 3: Self-Reflection	Step 7	Step 8		
Level 4: Self-Monitoring	Step 9	Step 10		

The steps in each level become automatic to you – they become common practice and become embedded as habits in time.

STEPS IN SELF-MENTORING

STEP 1: **Talents and Avoidances**
You become familiar with and identify talents and avoidances in your environment, the people in your environment, and YOURSELF.

STEP 2: **Expectations, Expectations, and   Expectations!**
You identify an expectation after compiling a list of potential options. Write down the expectation so that others could understand it if they were to read it.

STEP 3: **Strategic Thinking**
Once you have your expectation, you develop measurable strategy(s). A strategy is an activity that can be used to gather data that drives your efforts.

STEP 4: **Mixing and Measuring**
The strategy must be measurable either quantitatively, qualitatively or a through mixture of both. You may count for frequency or observe for behaviors.

STEP 5: **Timing is Everything**
Establish a timeline during which you collect the data. Include a beginning and ending. Plan for each day or each week as you implement the strategy and collect data until you reach the end of your timeline.

STEP 6: **Collecting and Sorting**
Data are your best friend. Collect data from your activities whether it is in the form of videotape or an observation from a colleague. Collect feedback from the activity. It may be you watching a video and making notes or a comparison of your notes with several colleagues who provided feedback on the same video. You may collect observation notes from several colleagues for feedback.

Level 3

STEP 7: <u>Reaching Out</u>
You will want to consider internal and external networking to set up a self-mentoring team, reach out to experts in the field or more experienced individuals for advice, and/or reach out to just a few trusting peers for feedback and reflection time.

STEP 8: <u>Making Sense of It All</u>
Once you have collected data from various activities and have feedback from identified sources, then time can be spent to really reflect on what the data is telling you. *What does it mean?*

Level 4

STEP 9: <u>Reflection Time</u>
After reviewing the data, you may want to reflect upon what you have learned and apply it to the situation to test your solutions. *Did it work? Why or why not?*

STEP 10: <u>Keep Your Eye on the Ball</u>
Monitor your accomplishment. You may want to develop a periodic status check. If embedded, then you may consider starting a new expectation and repeating the process.

Chapter Summary

Self-Mentoring is a four-level process in which skills are built and developed at each level. The four levels are: *Self-Awareness; Self-Development; Self-Reflection;* and *Self-Monitoring.* Each level applies skills learned in the previous level. While there is a structure to the practice, you individualize the process; it is unique to only you. You begin to alter your habits, develop new patterns of behavior, and/or change your present situation as you incorporate the ten steps of self-mentoring in your life. *It is your life; you must lead!*

Self and Peer-Reflection Activities

- *Select a friend and describe in detail each of the four levels of Self-Mentoring.*
- *Review each of the four levels and determine what will be your greatest challenge in preparation for Self-Mentoring.*
- *Isolate each level and review the steps to reach the next level.*
- *Rate your confidence in each level. Are some levels more challenging than others?*
- *Determine the levels that you believe you are going to need more support and determine what resources are available to you in your present situation.*

4

The Self-Awareness Level

"A man who doubts himself is like a man who would enlist in the ranks of his enemies and bear arms against himself. He makes his failure certain by himself being the first person to be convinced of it."

- *Alexandre Dumas, fils*

Let's begin the first level in Self-Mentoring – Self-Awareness - in which you will learn about your environment and YOU. There are *internal* and *external* factors in your environment that you will learn to recognize as they relate to and influence your organization, those in the organization, and YOU (Figure 1.8).

Figure 1.8: Level 1-Self-Awareness

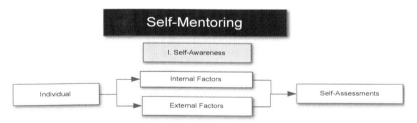

Your Environment

The second you walk into a new environment, you are surrounded by clues. You need to learn to recognize these clues just like an investigator walks onto a crime scene or a crash site looking for evidence. You must operate as a detective and awaken your sense of awareness. Put on your sleuth hat and grab your investigative pad (or iPad). Think about the opening scenario in Chapter 1 and the clues available to you during your first day on the job in a new environment. Use the following questions to guide your reflection.

EXTERIOR

- *What was your reaction to the exterior of the building upon arrival?*
- *Were there signs to guide you to parking?*
- *Was ample parking available?*
- *Were certain parking spaces designated as belonging to those in charge?*
- *Was your arrival organized?*
- *Did you feel safe when entering the building?*
- *Was the building well maintained and was the setting aesthetically pleasing?*
- *Were the grounds clean and free of trash?*
- *Was it inviting or confusing?*

If the environment is welcoming and inviting, then your path to acclimation could be easier to navigate. If you observe potential obstacles at first glance, it could be a warning sign or a false alarm. Let's continue our investigation as we enter the organization.

Environment
- *Did someone greet you or were you on your own?*
- *Were there visible displays to honor the organizations' successes such as awards, banners, or an employee-of-the-month wall?*
- *How friendly were the new colleagues that you encountered upon your first arrival?*
- *Was your induction organized or not?*
- *Was someone offered to serve as a mentor?*

Those in the Environment
- *Did you observe friendly banter or professional exchanges between the employees or personnel?*
- *How were other employees greeted upon arrival?*
- *Do the employees seem friendly and respectful of each other?*
- *Are the employees serious and steadfast in their routines?*
- *Is there chaos and confusion? Or organization and structure? Or both?*
- *Do you feel like you want to work there on first impression?*

The above internal and external observations are only a snapshot of the organization. They may or may not reflect the organization as a whole. But the clues you uncover upon your first arrival can be critical in understanding your organization. Even if you have been working at the same organization for years, you should pause and reflect upon your environment as if you were seeing it for the first time. Organizations are not static; they are fluid and shift constantly. So, the organization you came into several years ago may not be the same organization that you are in at present. And it may shift again. This is not uncommon. Over time, my organization shifted into an inspiring culture, but it could shift again. You assess your surroundings in order to answer the previous questions. Think back to your first encounter. *What was it like? How did you feel? How do you feel now? Have your feelings changed from the time you began?*

Ed Catmull, President of PIXAR Animation Studios, explains in a PIXAR University YouTube video how he blended the creative culture of Hollywood with the high-tech culture of Silicon Valley to create one of the most innovative training programs in the United States and perhaps the world. Steve Jobs, former CEO, confessed that the task of blending these two diverse groups into what they referred to as the 'PIXAR culture' was a significant challenge. When it came to merging these teams of creative and innovative designers, PIXAR took training seriously. They developed the PIXAR University for budding new hires to spark the genius in each of them by enrolling them in courses such as drawing, live action, painting, sculpture, color theory, and animation. While taking such classes, PIXAR employees were immersed in the creative culture and provided with the necessary skills to promote company success. They learned to work together as teams and to support each other and their respective crafts; hence, their work supported the company

The key to the success of the PIXAR University is the 'social bonding', which often doesn't occur in work environments. Students at the university learn project expertise as well as respect for others with complementary skills, in order to complete the projects. Those that work at PIXAR are encouraged to be innovative, dress comfortably, and stimulate creativity.

At first glance, walking into PIXAR could be a mix of chaos and distraction. But after careful observation, it might be viewed as a stimulating and innovative environment. Looks can be deceiving. Make careful note of details when you enter an environment, either mentally or visually, in order to reflect upon them later. These details become important.

Conversations and Collaborations

Conversations are crucial in every profession. They are a powerful tool that enables understanding and comradery within an organization. (Patterson, Grenny, McMillan, & Switzler, 2012). Conversation is equally important in self-mentoring. Through the identification of key employees or personnel in the new environment, the history and culture of the organization can be discovered. Topics may include turnover of leaders, political factions, current operating procedures, present system-wide leadership, personnel expectations, and the chemistry of the community or clientele-at-large. Meeting peers in the work environment can serve to identify the internal hierarchies of power. The following questions should help guide your inquiry:

- *Who represents the best model of a leader in your organization?*
- *What political factions exist? Can they be avoided? Or are they an obstacle?*
- *Who can you trust? How will you determine whom you can trust?*
- *Who should you avoid? Why? How will you avoid these individuals?*
- *Who is really in charge? Is he or she approachable?*
- *Are decisions transparent or made without input?*
- *What is encouraged and what is not?*

Power, relations, networks, and politics all play an important role in your efforts. Some personnel may be friendly and others guarded. Some personnel will share leadership roles and others will hoard power or steal ideas. Knowing the areas of expertise that your colleagues possess can serve as a valuable resource for you. Maintaining a mental library of resource specialists available to you in the organization is especially important for new employees. Those in the organization adept at a specific skill or serving in positive leadership roles understand the climate and are often willing to have conversations about the functionality of the organization. Collaborations are born from these encounters, establishing meaningful relationships. This can become your lifeline in the organization. Some additional questions are provided that may be helpful.

- *Are value statements or mission/vision statements posted visibly for everyone to observe?*
- *Are these statements respected?*
- *What is the history of the organization in regard to leadership? Has there been frequent turnover of leaders and/or employees?*
- *Is there diversity among the staff? Is diversity welcomed?*
- *Are employees helpful to each other?*
- *Are ideas shared or kept guarded/secret?*
- *Are different genders respected and treated equally?*
- *Is there a designated area for staff to visit or have lunch? Is it encouraged?*
- *Is collaboration encouraged or independent thinking?*
- *What incentives are in place or are you expected to be self-motivated?*
- *How are employees valued?*

In the space on the following page, write an overview of your organization from your experiences, conversations, and observations. An example is also provided.

Sample Organization
My organization is welcoming and inviting. The people are respectful of each other and friendly. They greet each other with smiles and talk politely about personal and professional events. However, in private conversations I am warned to guard my ideas – not because they will be stolen but because it will anger others who may not feel as successful.

YOUR Organization

It also is important to identify skills that you think you must possess to function effectively in your environment. Examples of skills you may need include: *organization, honesty, being personable, friendly, being a good communicator, having the capacity to work alone, being able to complete a task, being a leader, creativity, innovation, being a team builder, and/or possessing strong speaking, writing, or computer skills.* List the skills that you feel you need on the following page. You will refine this list during activities in another level.

Organizational Skills

1. _____

2. _____

3. _____

4. _____

5. _____

Knowing your environment and those in your environment is 50% of the challenge in learning to be successful. Knowing YOU is the other half.

YOU

So, who are you? What are your talents? What are your assets? What are your challenges or avoidances that get in your way? It is important for you to be able to look in the mirror and see you for who you are as well as what you can contribute to an organization.

- *What kind of employee are you?*
- *What are your greatest assets as an employee?*
- *Do people respect you or fear you?*
- *How do you lead when you are in charge of others?*
- *How do other people see you? Are you honest? Are you dependable?*
- *Are you creative or innovative in making decisions?*
- *Are you a hard worker? Do you meet deadlines or quotas?*
- *Do you care what others think of you? Or does it not matter?*

- *Most importantly, would you hire you as an employee if this were your organization? Why?*
- *Are you calm and thoughtful? Are you needy or attention seeking?*
- *Do you strengthen the organization as part of a team or work solo?*

Defining Leadership

What exactly is leadership? If we think of a fingerprint left on a glass, it is identification unique to one individual. Like the swirls, curves, and twirled marks of a fingerprint identify one individual from another, so each decision and attitude of a leader marks the significant attributes in their leadership. That is why leadership is one of the most observed and least understood phenomena on earth (Wren, 1995) and this still holds true today. Self-mentoring adheres to the belief that leadership is not an exact science, but an individualized process, unique to each individual.

Leadership is not a conclusion, but a process, an evolution, a relationship between the environment, situations, individuals, and social interactions that are much too complex to isolate and package as 'one size fits all' (Lambert, 2003). Great leaders are bred from great causes. But leaders, at their best, also breed great causes, according to Hesselbein, Goldsmith, and Beckhard (1997). The authors also believe that leadership grows out of courage and integrity, a seed found in everyone. Courage is defined as the ability to do what needs to be done, regardless of the risk or cost, and integrity is defined as the ability to do the right thing (Hesselbein, et. al.). It takes confidence to exhibit courage. Self-mentoring focuses on building confidence and embraces the tenet that, given the right opportunity, the leader in each of us will emerge.

Your Leadership Fingerprint

Learning how to recognize your strengths and avoidances initially seems as simple as developing a to-do or shopping list. It can be that easy or it can be more complex. There are a variety of assessments and activities that can be used to assist in the identification of your leadership traits. Kiersey.com is a free website that provides a tool to assess your style of leadership. Kiersey provides individual leadership assessment, and a team analysis is also available for users. Additional leadership inventories and activities are listed at the end of this chapter, which you may use to explore and gain insight into your leadership style. The inventories and activities at the end of the chapter are a fun way to capture snapshots of characteristics you possess. But as in most leadership inventories, this is just a glimpse of your potential.

Now YOU begin with the following self-mentoring activity. In the following space, identify what you believe to be your strengths and an example (or indicator) of why these characteristics are strengths. You might write that your *ability to organize* is a strength and the indicator is that you *enjoy or are capable of juggling multiple tasks daily*. Or you may list your strength as *creativity* and the indicator is that you are *able to find multiple solutions for any challenge*. Now it is your turn to complete this exercise using the chart on the following page. An example is also provided.

SAMPLE Leadership Strengths
Honest
Outspoken
Courageous
Articulate
Sincere
Ethical
Trustworthy
Organized
Visionary
Communicator
Responsible
Logical
Decision-maker
Displays common sense
Humorous
Intelligent

Your Leadership Strengths

Strength	Indicators (evidence)

Once you have completed the exercise, list your strengths as a leader once again in the following chart.

MY Leadership Strengths

Using the list you have compiled of your leadership strengths, rank each item, beginning with your greatest strength as #1, until you have ranked all the characteristics in a hierarchal order. The following chart is provided to assist you.

Rank Order of Leadership Strengths

Rank	Leadership Strength

Then, without sharing your ranked list of strengths, use your *MY Leadership Strengths* chart to ask several friends or co-workers, whom you trust to be candid, to complete the same exercise and rank your strengths. You may encourage them to list additional strengths they believe you possess that have been omitted from the list or you could ask them to develop their own list without sharing the list you developed. The activity can be as flexible as you desire. You want insight into how others view you as a leader.

Once you have collected several lists from your friends or co-workers, list the results in the following chart in order to compare the feedback from colleagues/friends with your own assessment.

Colleague Ranking of Leadership Strengths

Rank Comparison				
Strength	Colleague 1	Colleague 2	Colleague 3	YOUR Rank

This becomes an important part of learning about YOU. Often we do not see ourselves as others do. We can be much more harsh on ourselves. We can learn so much about ourselves from the perspective of those around us. It is often shocking, but it can also be affirming. An example of a completed chart is provided on the following page.

Colleague Ranking of Leadership Strengths

Rank Comparison				
Strength	Colleague 1	Colleague 2	Colleague 3	YOUR Rank
Honest	3	4	3	1
Organized	2	3	1	4
Responsible	4	2	2	2
Trust-worthy	6	5	4	3
Intelligent	5	1	6	6
Communicator	1	6	5	5

As you review the chart above, the results are different for each person that completed the ranking. There are several ways to begin to sort this type of data and a more detailed overview of how to sort data will be explored in the next chapter, but some common techniques to aggregate this information are:

1) Add each line for an average to rank the characteristics, or
2) Establish a middle of 5 if you have ten characteristics or 3 if you have six. Then determine if each characteristic primarily falls above the line or below the line. This gives you a general idea of importance.

There are other leadership activities you can apply that will be equally effective in collecting meaningful data about YOU as a leader. Some additional activities have been provided.

- Distribute a video device and ask co-workers or friends to make a short video (no more than three minutes) explaining what characteristics you possess as a leader.
- Start a paragraph with one sentence about you and ask others to contribute one sentence until you build a paragraph that describes you as a leader.

- Ask your colleagues or friends to select only one word that they think best embodies you as a leader.

The purpose of the exercises is to provide a platform for you to understand the skills you may not be aware you possess and highlight those you do. As previously written, we often need affirmation from others to tap into our potential only because we fail to recognize our own strengths. Once you have completed several exercises and feel that you understand your strengths, write them down in a narrative format in the box provided and refer back to them to remind yourself of your abilities. An example is provided.

Sadie's Leadership Strengths

I am an <u>honest</u>, <u>hard-working</u>, <u>responsible</u>, and <u>organized</u> leader that believes the role of a leader is to serve others. I like to <u>inspire</u> others and see them reach their full potential. I use <u>humor</u> to make uncomfortable situations comfortable along with <u>common sense</u> and <u>creativity</u> to problem-solve.

Now write your own leadership story in the following space. Underline your strengths in the narrative.

My Leadership Strengths

As you begin to recognize the leader in YOU, we move to the next step in self-mentoring. We set expectations as this chapter closes and Level 1 concludes.

Expectations

Expectation, as related to self-mentoring, is the belief that you can achieve something worthy of obtaining. It could be to reach a level of performance or successfully complete a project but the expectation must be believable, realistic, and attainable with maximum effort by YOU. It may be an expectation of something you expect to change or alter. It can be your intent - what you expect to achieve or a level of success you aspire to reach. The point is that it is YOUR expectation.

Begin by listing all the expectations that come to mind, in no particular order. Any expectation that you have can be listed. Just begin writing for several minutes, unclouded with other thoughts, or start the list and then return to it day after day until you feel it is complete. You may want to begin by asking yourself, *what is working in your life? What is not working?* The challenges may or may not be transparent or known, but take time to reflect on the challenges you face that are currently blocking your progress or success. An expectation often develops from challenges. It doesn't matter how you arrive at a list, just create a meaningful and realistic list of expectations for YOU.

Write your expectations on the following chart that has been provided. There is space for ten expectations but don't focus on the number, just list the number of expectations that represent you.

Sometimes the more you list, the easier it becomes to isolate or focus on one expectation later. As you develop your list, you may find that some of the expectations are very broad and can be broken down from large intentions into easy to achieve tasks. Use the *Breakdown into smaller* column in the chart for this purpose, if needed. An example is provided to demonstrate a broad theme with smaller components that may be appropriate for setting an expectation.

Sample Expectation Chart

	Expectation List	Breakdown into smaller components if feasible.
1	*I expect to be a more recognized leader at work.*	*-Increased leadership roles* *-Committee leadership roles* *-Volunteer for positions* *-Make my desire to lead known if appropriate*

Expectations Chart

	Expectation List	Breakdown into smaller components if feasible.
1		
2		

3		
4		
5		
6		
7		
8		
9		
10		

Once you develop a list of potential expectations, you must narrow the list to just one expectation that will become your focus. An example has been provided.

Sadie's Expectation
I expect to be able to organize my day so that I have personal time for working out or walking in the evenings or even reading novels.

Write the expectation you have determined in the following space. It is important to write the expectation as a statement so you can refer back to it from time to time.

Expectation

Challenges of the Environment

You must learn how to confront or overcome obstacles that block your path in achieving the expectation you set for YOU. These challenges are the norm and there are manageable ways to maneuver through what may feel like an obstacle course. There are a number of significant challenges that can serve as obstacles in your career path, which include, but may not be limited to the following:

- Getting oriented to the environment or setting
- Finding a collegial or external friend and ally
- Understanding how to balance the need to achieve and need to please
- Creating a balance between professional roles and also between your personal life
- Managing the expectations for successful performance

- Underachieving or Overachieving
- Eliminating actions that alienate other staff
- Dealing with difficult people or bullies in the workplace
- Learning how to meet the expectations of any required tasks or jobs
- Organizing yourself or managing your time

As you review the preceding list, write down any obstacles that you believe exist that could prevent you from meeting your expectation in the following space. Why do the obstacle(s) exist and what can you do to eliminate the obstacle(s) in your environment?

Your Obstacles

1. _____
2. _____
3. _____
4. _____
5. _____

Select the most critical obstacle and write a passage about how you will work to resolve this obstacle in the following space provided. You will have other opportunities to work on obstacles but this list is a start. You might re-visit this list and add new obstacles as they are discovered along your journey.

Resolving the Obstacle

Chapter Summary

This chapter serves to assist you in getting started as a self-mentor. It is the process of looking in the mirror to assess your own capabilities and the needs of the organization you serve or are going to serve. You learn about your leadership strengths and look in mirror to assess your own reflection as well as to see how others view you as a leader. Within these reflections, you begin to formulate a plan that will increase your success in the organization.

Self and Peer-Reflection Activities

- *Write a paragraph that reflects your assessment of the external features of an organization.*
- *Write a paragraph that reflects your assessment of the individuals in the organization.*
- *Write a paragraph describing yourself as a leader. Ask friends to read your paragraph and react to your assessment. Use this feedback to compare and contrast your assessment with those of friends who know you well.*
- *Compare your strengths as a leader to those necessary to succeed in your organization.*
- *Develop an expectation for your focus as a self-mentor. Share your plan with others for reactions and suggestions.*

Leadership Activities and Interactive Games:
http://www.workshopexercises.com/Leadership.htm

Young Adult Leadership site:
http://www.ehow.com/list_6528308_interactive-leadership-games.html

Leadership activities:
http://schlags.com/paul/leadership/listing1zx4ja8ch8.php
http://www.buzzle.com/articles/interactive-leadership-activities.html
http://leadership.uoregon.edu/resources/exercises_tips
http://www.what-are-good-leadership-skills.com/activities-for-leadership-workshops.html
http://www.thiagi.com/games.html

Additional Resources:
Keirsey Individual and Group Leadership sorter http://www.keirsey.com
The Leadership Challenge (Inventory for adults and students)
http://www.leadershipchallenge.com/leaders-section-assessments.aspx
Personal Leadership Inventory (teams, individuals, students)
http://www.skillsusa.org/educators/pli.shtml

Student Leadership Practices Inventory® 360 (students)
http://www.studentleadershipchallenge.com/UserFiles/Sample_Student_LPI_360_Online_Individual_Report.pdf

5

The Self-Development Level

"Self-confidence is the first requisite to great undertakings."

- *Samuel Johnson*

In the second level of self-mentoring, you formulate your plan. You re-visit your expectation that you wrote at the end of Level 1 and you develop a plan built on an expectation – YOUR expectation. At any time, you should be able to recite your expectation from memory.

The following diagram (Figure 1.9) outlines the process. You will select strategies, develop a timeline, determine appropriate measurements, and learn to form an assessment from this data.

Figure 1.9: Level 2 - Self-Development

Begin by writing your expectation from memory in the space below. You need to know your expectation without referring to notes. It is key to your plan.

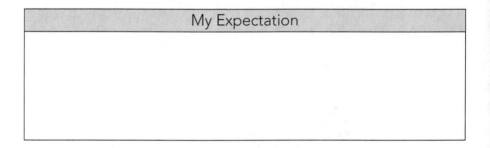

Once you write your expectation, you will begin developing strategies to achieve your expectation.

Strategy Development

Strategies are small steps in the process to collect information or data. You can begin by assessing your current situation. List the potential strategies below that would help you meet your expectation in the *Strategy* column of the following chart.

Developing Strategies

	Strategy	Measurement
1		
2		
3		
4		
5		
6		

Now that you have listed strategies, you will begin to consider the types of measurement available for each strategy to collect information. Technology can play an important role in this, decreasing time and energy by using available tools.

Incorporating Technology

The use of technology is always a consideration in organization. There are a multitude of devices and software to assist you in sorting and collecting data as well as monitoring future data. Technology can serve to expedite data collection and analysis in addition to displaying the data in a way that is visually interpretative and meaningful. Some examples are as follows:

- Excel spreadsheets to chart data
- Timelines such as Dipity.com for monitoring
- Microsoft word charts
- Outlook Calendar for organizing

- Electronic journals for notes
- LiveBinders.com (Organizational folders)
- Apps developed specifically for self-mentoring

The *Self-mentoring app* is designed to compliment the four levels and guide you through the process using electronic clues. While not a requirement for project completion, it is available at http://www.selfmentoring.net.

As you progress through each level and develop a plan for implementation, you will be able to distinguish what technologies are best suited for your individual needs and organize accordingly. There are also a variety of tools for measurement that can assist in the process.

Measurement

Each strategy that you listed in the previous chart must be measurable. Questions you should ask are:

- *What type of information can I collect from each strategy?*
- *What type of information do I need to collect?*
- *What type of information do I want to collect?*
- *How will I know if the strategy is working or is successful?*
- *What will the collected information tell me?*
- *What do I need to measure the success of the strategy?*
- *What types of information are best for specific situations?*

You can measure the strategies qualitatively or quantitatively. You can even use a mixture of both. Each measurement is suitable for specific situations. The difficulty will be in aligning the most appropriate measurement with your strategy, so careful consideration needs to be given in selecting your measurement.

Qualitative data is difficult to count and more interpretative in nature. Observations, interviews, or personal reflections are often qualitative in nature. These data are collected through notes, journals, dialog, or other written sources that allow for elucidation. This type of information is not easily counted or quantified, but is more subjective in nature, allowing for interpretation.

Quantitative data is most often reported numerically by percentages, statistics, or numerations. Often surveys, questionnaires, or other instruments are used to collect this type of data. It can also be observable. If you count the number of repetitions in a given situation, count a show of hands, or rank items in a list, this is quantitative. Obviously, this is an oversimplification of a very complex process but for your purposes, you only need to touch the surface of measurement in order to benefit from the results.

Mixed data collection involves a combination of both qualitative and quantitative measurement. A more detailed overview of data collection is provided at the end of this chapter for reference.

The following questions may also be helpful in the process.

- *Are you going to be <u>counting the number of times </u>something occurs?*
- *Are you going to be <u>using observations and notes</u>?*
- *Are you <u>using feedback </u>from others to compare with your own reflection notes?*
- *Are you <u>monitoring</u> an action?*
- *Are you <u>observing</u> a behavior?*
- *Are you <u>using checkpoints </u>to monitor or observe a behavior?*
- *Are you capturing video to look for <u>patterns</u>?*

- Are you <u>comparing</u> behaviors or items?
- Are you <u>mapping or plotting an occurrence</u>?

You have listed strategies in the *Strategy* column on the previous chart; now complete the *Measurement* column.

Developing A Measurable Strategy

	Strategy	Measurement
1		
2		
3		
4		
5		
6		

From your strategy and measurement list in the chart, isolate one or two strategies that are best suited to meet your expectation. The strategy guides the type of measurement you need to use in collecting data. There are some examples on page 79. If you find this challenging, share your vision with a colleague or friend to gain additional insight. You may want to share your work with others for feedback even if you feel you have developed a measurable strategy. Write the strategy as a sentence or paragraph in the space below, including how you will measure the strategy.

Strategy

Teams and Networking

Garvey (2014) believes it is not mentoring alone that improves individual performance, but team support also influences it. Self-mentoring improves performance through individual effort and individual networking to build team support. While self-mentoring implies self, it doesn't mean that you do it *all* yourself. It does mean that you do accept responsibility for your progress. Your progress is often reliant on feedback and reflections from others. You cannot underestimate the need to build and surround yourself with a strong team of individuals that you trust and who exhibit the level of expertise needed to support your growth. It becomes important to select those that you trust and can cultivate meaningful relationships with to augment your efforts. Self-mentors become experts at developing pools of individuals who are valuable resources in any environment. These individuals can provide feedback, peer-reflection time, and even guidance when necessary. As you are working on the development and implementation of your plan, develop a team of individuals that become your support. As you build your team, list them in the following space.

Self-Mentoring Team	
Name	Support

Your team is critical but may change over time. As your needs change, the list may also change to adapt to your needs.

Building a Timeline

Time has to be set aside for self-mentoring. The time should align with the needs of your expectation. To be successful, you need to be considerate of the time you dedicate for each activity or are willing to spend based on your workload and schedule. You should be able to address the following questions.

- *How much time are you willing to schedule for self-mentoring activities?*
- *How much time are you willing to devote to activities that will provide data?*
- *How much time are you willing to dedicate to observations and technological viewings?*
- *How much time are you willing to schedule for self-mentoring reflections with other colleagues?*
- *How much time are you willing to schedule for your personal growth?*

Begin by dedicating time for your strategy and complete an actual timeline devoted to your strategy implementation and measurement. You may prefer to use online calendars instead of the following calendar and timeline that has been provided. The key is to use whatever device you are comfortable with, a devise that can provide a means to schedule the time you are devoting to meet your expectation.

My Self-Mentoring Calendar						
Sun	Mon	Tues	Wed	Thurs	Fri	Sat

You can use a calendar format or you can use a timeline as provided below. Remember there are many electronic timelines accessible as provided earlier in this chapter.

Timeline

_____

The following questions may guide you in the process of developing a timeline.

- *How much time do you need to adequately capture data to assess or evaluate your efforts?*
- *Are you gathering data daily or are you collecting data over a longer period of time?*
- *How will you collect data during this time period?*
- *Do you need time to meet with others and get feedback?*
- *Are their seasonal or job-related conflicts to work around?*
- *How will you know if you have a realistic snapshot of data?*
- *Do you need to build in an extension beyond the timeline for any unexpected interruptions?*

Self-mentoring works best when implemented for two to eight weeks, although adjustments can be made based on feedback and continuous planning. Your self-mentoring plan is fluid and forms to your individual needs, so if your needs change, you alter your plan. It is that simple.

A blank guide is provided on the following page to help organize your self-mentoring plan, focusing on the key components. The blank guide has sections you have previously completed in this chapter and you can complete by filling in steps (1-6) in the chart. A sample plan has also been provided that was developed by an exceptional-needs teacher who was working in a public school setting and struggling to reach out to classroom teachers. She developed a self-mentoring plan to collaborate with core content education teachers. If you are able to complete the chart, you are on your way to building your self-mentoring plan.

Sample Self-mentoring Planning Guide:

Self-mentoring™ Guide

Step	Actions	Your Plan
1	YOUR Expectation	I will improve my case management skills.
2	What Presently Doing	*Assumption:* Present data tracking system is not effective.
3	What Works? Doesn't?	*Assumption:* Present data tracking system is not providing data needed or is meaningful.
4	New strategy time.	**Strategy: Find new data tracker for IEP goals that is more effective.** *1. Talk to other EC teachers about how they track data. 2. Have someone else look at how I track data. 3. Create my own data tracking system if unable to find one.*
5	Build Timeline (2-4 wks.)	**1. Talk to other EC teachers about how they track data. 2. Have someone else look at how presently track data. 3. Select different systems to try over a period of time – 2-4 weeks for data.**
6	Measure! Measure! Measure!	**1. Review feedback from other's observations. 2. Review feedback from reflection with others. 3. Consider ratings of effectiveness from different system that you tried.**

Self-mentoring™ Guide

Step	Actions	Your Plan
1	YOUR Expectation	
2	What Presently Doing	
3	What Works? Doesn't?	
4	New Strategy time!	
5	Build Timeline (2-4 wks.)	
6	Measure! Measure! Measure!	

Reflection Time

Self-mentoring embraces the need to self-reflect and use peer-reflection time. This is central to the practice – an ethos of the art. Reflection can include facilitated conversations or casual discussions. Without these conversations, we cannot think new thoughts nor develop new thoughts about old ideas, customs, or practices (Fullan, 2008).

Mentoring programs typically schedule weekly meetings with the mentor and mentee in and out of the work environment to discuss the status of efforts. You are self-mentoring so you will not be scheduling time to meet someone; however, you do have to schedule time to review the status of your efforts. In addition, you must do this without someone encouraging or reminding you about it. You have to be self-motivated in scheduling this time. You could think of it as having a meeting with yourself. As humorous as it may sound, when a Limited Liability Company (LLC), with only one owner, conducts a meeting for tax purposes, the owner is the only person in attendance yet minutes are kept to reflect the activity and the sole individual in attendance. Think of yourself as the single business owner, devoted to the success of your company. The following questions will guide your agenda.

- *What are the priorities that need to be considered?*
- *What are the next steps to meet your expectation?*
- *What obstacles still exist?*
- *What can be done to overcome any existing challenges?*
- *Is your plan realistic?*
- *What adjustments might need to be made?*
- *What would you hope to get out of the meeting?*
- *How will you know if you have met your expectation?*

- *What constitutes acceptable progress?*

You can record or take notes during your meetings. This becomes helpful in tracking your progress. You don't always have to meet alone. You can schedule meetings with your self-mentoring team or a member of the team when needed. This could be a lunch or even dinner meeting. Use the following calendar, or an electronic version, to schedule reflection or peer-reflection time to discuss your progress.

My Self-Mentoring Calendar						
Sun	Mon	Tues	Wed	Thurs	Fri	Sat

You are well on your way to implementing your plan to self-mentor. In the next level of self-mentoring, you will implement your plan, collect data, analyze the information, and critique your feedback.

Chapter Summary

From this chapter we learned how to develop measurable strategies to meet your expectation. The type of measurement that will be used for collecting data has been determined and you are ready for implementation using a timeline to chart data collection. You now have a plan for implementation. You are ready to begin self-mentoring.

Self or Peer-Reflection Activities

- *Share you expectation with a colleague or friend. Be prepared to answer any questions they may have about your expectation.*
- *Reflect on a few strategies that you could use to collect information regarding the success of your efforts to self-mentor.*
- *Share your self-mentoring plan with colleagues for feedback.*
- *Set up some reflection time with others to talk about your self-mentoring plan.*
- *Write your plan repeatedly so you are comfortable with what you have set out to measure.*

Measurement Methods

Qualitative:
- Peer-Reflection notes
- Narrative feedback
- Self-Reflection journals
- Video observations
- Audio tape notes
- Interviews
- Conversations
- Log books
- Journal entries

Quantitative:
- Numerical counts
- Numbered lists
- Patterns
- Repetitions
- Hierarchies
- Rankings
- Selections
- Scales

Mixed Methods (combinations of any of the above):
- Scales and video observations
- Show of hands for a count and conversations
- Interview notes and ranked lists

6

The Self-Reflection Level

"They are able who think they are able."

- Virgil

The third level in self-mentoring is Self-Reflection in which you learn to self-reflect and use peer-reflection. This chapter encompasses collecting data, feedback, reflection, networking, and data analysis as shown in the illustration below (Figure 1.10).

Figure 1.10: Level 3 - Self-reflection

To begin, in the space below, write a summary of your plan, without referring to any previous notes, so that a friend unfamiliar with self-mentoring could understand your plan to meet your expectation. Be sure to include *what you are doing, how you will do it, when you will do it, how long you will do it, what you will measure, how you will measure it, and why you are doing it.* Yes, all in one paragraph.

My Self-Mentoring Plan

Your plan is now ready for implementation. Select a day and time that is best suited for you to begin. You may choose to postpone collecting data until you have set up any necessary staging. Some examples of self-mentoring plans have been provided.

Taylor works for a corporation in the United States. The company produces consumable products. She is the manager of a department that controls the marketing of each of these products. Data is collected and shared at meetings to gauge the success of each product. Taylor is struggling with an employee that is borderline disrespectful to her during these meetings. She never has enough evidence to support insubordination and for the most part, this individual had great ideas. She doesn't want to reprimand the person, but instead, wishes for this person to become more polite and respectful of others.

Taylor begins self-mentoring. She develops the following plan. The necessary components of this plan are identified in parenthesis.

Taylor's Self-mentoring Plan
I expect that I will develop skills to work with individuals I encounter in meeting (Who) who need support (What) so that I can assist them without distractions that ultimately hinder my performance (Why). I will begin by collecting information. For two weeks, beginning next week (When) at work (Where), I am going to chart each time I find myself upset with this or similar employees (How). I will log the duration of the occurrence, write a brief overview, and use a scale from 1-5 that ranks how upset I am (1 as the lowest reaction and 5 as the highest level of disruption) on a chart. I want to know the % of time lost to these distractions and the degree of anxiety.

Taylor collected data and compiled it in the following chart. In the chart, she monitored the daily interruptions with a length of time (M = amount in minutes) and 1-5 scale for each event (L = Level of intensity).

Taylor's Individual Disruption Chart

Week 1	Day 1	Day 2	Day 3	Day 4	Day 5
175 M L 2, 3, 4, 5	10 / L3 5 / L2	NA	120 / L5	30 / L4	10 / L4
Week 2	**Day 6**	**Day 7**	**Day 8**	**Day 9**	**Day 10**
35 M L 2, 3, 4	NA	5 / L2	5 / L3 5 / L4 5 / L2	10 / L3	10 / L3

Taylor also kept a log that detailed each of the events for self-reflection. The following is an example of her log entry.

Taylor's Log Book

Day 3: Today we had a team meeting. Kevin was disruptive and all but argued with me over an idea. The team looks at me as if I should be control and I am trying to use patience. It is the way that Kevin handles situations that is the most frustrating. It feels as though he is doing it on purpose to make me look weak as the team leader. He challenged me on a project idea that was another team members' idea by pointing out all the reasons that we shouldn't use it but yet he has no idea to replace it. He wasted so much of my time and the team's today. The team could tell that I was frustrated.

Taylor reviewed her data. She saw that during her first week, she spent 175 minutes at Level 2-5 and during the second week, she spent 35 minutes at Level 2-4. Her second week was less distracting than the first. The first week was severe due to a half-day team meeting that was disrupted by another person's actions and Taylor's inability to stop it. Her log gives her insight into each situation so she can begin to look for patterns. Taylor knows she must get control of the situation. Her success depends on it. Another example is Jennings.

> Jennings' responsibilities require him to work on projects that often overlap and may take months to complete. He is concerned that he is not dedicating sufficient time to the perfect completion of each project and that his approach will, over time, cause him to appear to be less competent than he believes he is as a professional. Jennings begins self-mentoring and he develops a plan for his success.

I expect that I will learn how to manage multiple projects to perfection at work. Beginning immediately, I will mark sections of time on a calendar using backward mapping from the deadline for each project. I will include incremental checkpoints to monitor my progress and gather feedback on the success of each project. I will arrange the projects into a hierarchy based on their importance and then schedule one project at a time to ensure that sufficient time is available for each project.

Jennings is going to use mixed method data to measure his efforts. He is going to focus on completing specific tasks so he needs quantitative data from meeting specific checkpoints, but also qualitative data in feedback from outside resources.

- He will monitor the <u>successful completion of tasks at checkpoints</u> on his calendar.
- He will <u>record the time</u> he devoted to the project and the time it actually took to complete the project in detail.
- He will use colleagues to look over his product at each <u>checkpoint</u> to <u>get feedback</u> about the <u>quality of his work</u>.
- He will have colleagues read over his <u>final product</u> and ask them for feedback.

Jennings will schedule projects over a two-month span. Using a calendar, he begins color-coding each project. Jennings begins by scheduling his first priority among a list of projects and highlights the work time he estimates to complete the project, as well as the time to get feedback and make changes if necessary. Once he completes the first project, he then adds a second project. He soon realizes that he cannot continue to manage the number of projects he is assigned with success, but he continues using the calendar until his time is filled. He will collect data to see if his assessment of the time needed for project completion is accurate as this may alter his available time. He will make adjustments once he has some solid data for planning. The following illustration is an example of his planning using the calendar.

Illustration 1.2: Calendar Example

Mon	Tues	Wed	Thurs	Fri
Project 1		Project 2		
Project 2	Project 1	Project 1		
Reflection		Project 1	Get feedback	Reflection
				Deadline to complete

The following additional examples of self-mentoring plans will provide insight in planning. Remember, the key is obtaining reliable information with which to base your decisions and plan.

Consultant:
Lucy is a consultant and constantly is speaking before large groups/audiences. She feels like she could be a better public speaker and more articulate. She has watched numerous videos on YouTube and read books to improve her speaking skills, but to no avail. Lucy decides to use quantitative data collection. Her plan is as follows:
- She is going to videotape herself while speaking.
- She is going to isolate one skill that she wants to improve (i.e. stop saying '*humm*' between thoughts).

- She is going to use videotapes to <u>monitor her improvement</u> and <u>count the number of times</u> she hears '*humm*' as she speak.
- She will monitor for a <u>reduction of this behavior</u>.

<u>Real Estate Agent:</u>
Jeffrey is a real estate agent and must constantly be motivated to list homes and sell. He wants to find a way to increase his sales by listing more homes. Jeffrey decides to use quantitative data collection. He has been collecting data using a calendar and incremental dates as checkpoints to monitor his progress over a three-month period of time.
His plan is as follows:
- He is going to <u>list all the ways to solicit property</u> to list.
- He will create a visual <u>wall chart</u> with each item as a heading.
- Then he will begin <u>using the different techniques</u> as he finds potential homes to list.
- His goal is to use this list to establish a <u>number of homes under each of the headings</u>.
- He wants to <u>balance his use of each technique</u> so that he will alter his behavior to be more productive.

<u>Middle School Teacher:</u>
Kelly is a middle school teacher and she often recognizes that she does not engage her students as often as she should. Kelly decides that she will be using a mixed method to collect data. Her plan is as follows:
- She decides to survey her students to ascertain what <u>activities</u> they believed were <u>most engaging</u>.
- She reviews the survey data and uses the <u>top student ranked activity</u> to begin a trial run for two weeks.

- She implements the activity and <u>monitors student's work</u> to see if there is an increase in student completion, student participation, and successful completion.
- She <u>collects data and reflects/shares it with her students</u> so that they are involved in the process.

Data Analysis

As you implement your plan, you gather information. The data you collect is analyzed. In other words, you have to make sense of the information in order to determine the next step – in other words, what you will do with the data.

Think back to Taylor's example. She was frustrated with an employee in her department and her data indicated that she was losing valuable time and energy, which limited her productivity. Taylor identified that the time lost was more significant and destructive than she originally anticipated. She developed her plan to tackle this obstacle in her workplace and to ensure her future success.

Taylor's Self-mentoring Action Plan

I am going to research some basic techniques for working with complicated employees. I will employ these techniques and begin trying them, one by one, to see which is most effective depending on my needs. I will rate the effectiveness of each strategy through the same process in collecting the original data. Once I identify the best technique(s), I am going to employ these techniques to lessen the time spent with a difficult employee, recognizing that I can't always change the behavior of others, but I can change my reaction to unwanted behaviors.

Taylor will continue to collect data and feedback until she has perfected the situation to either eliminate the obstacle or lessen it to a degree that it is not hindering her success.

Jennings, another self-mentor, was concerned about the quality of his projects. While he was completing projects, their quality was subpar, and he knew his reputation would eventually suffer if he did not alter the present situation. Jennings ascertained that, upon review of his data, he was not devoting sufficient time to any one project. In order to complete a project to perfection, he will build in checkpoints for feedback, using backward mapping from the deadline. Feedback was essential in making necessary changes. This is Jennings' plan.

Jennings' Self-mentoring Action Plan

I have realized that I need to devote more attention to my projects and build in quality feedback and reflection time. I will use my office calendar to block out sufficient time for each project, beginning with the most important, until sufficient time is allotted and then move onto the next project. As projects are assigned to me, I will continue to add them to the calendar but over time, I will be able to respond with an accurate assessment of my available time for completing projects with quality. This will also guarantee that I am looked at in a professional light as an organized and thorough designer. It is my desire to maintain a respected position among peers and other leaders.

Using the chart on the following page, list the data you collected and what you intend to do with the data. If you prefer to write it out, a narrative box has also been provided. Keep in mind that you may be collecting data on more than one occasion so if you use the charts, duplicate as many times as needed.

Data Collection Overview

Date of Collection	Data Collected	How Data Used

Data Collection and Analysis Plan

Data Collection and Analysis Plan

Once you have collected data and determined how you will use the information, you interpret the information for additional planning. The following chart is an example where the data, quantitative, used a survey and scale to determine an item of greatest importance or priority.

Data Collection and Analysis

Data Collection	Data Analysis	Interpretation
Survey	Ranked order	Priority
Scale (1-10)	Highest to lowest	Priority
Calendar	Percentage	Percentage of time

The following blank chart is provided to showcase your data. You may not need all the lines that are provided.

Data Collection	Data Analysis	Interpretation

Data analysis is storytelling - you must take time to review data. Often, as individuals, we believe we know the answer or we pretend we are too busy to be concerned. We are not willing to look in the mirror to see what we are doing and how it impacts our environment. We may find that our actions are the obstacle or challenge in our environment. Your focus is not on changing others but in finding ways to change what we do have control over – our ability as a leader.

Chapter Summary

From this chapter we learned how to establish a plan for gathering reliable data. You will implement your plan over a period of time and collect information as it becomes available to you. Once you have collected information, you will sort it and analyze it to make decisions that will put you on the path to success. You may find that collecting data guides you to experimenting with solutions. The cycle continues as you collect feedback until you have a solid solution for any obstacle. You now begin to see that self-mentoring is a process of discovery using action and research to make sound decisions that impact our careers and future leadership positions.

Self and Peer-Reflection Activities

- Set up some reflection time with others to talk about your self-mentoring plan and what you hope to accomplish.
- Consider a timeline necessary to capture sufficient information to provide a realistic overview to the situation. Think about how long it should take to capture a snapshot of the situation that could be insightful.
- Select some colleagues, co-workers, or friends with whom you could share your data to reflect on the information. *Do you both see the same results? If not, why?*
- Consider the different types of data collection and what type would be the most beneficial for your given circumstance.

7

The Self-Monitoring Level

"Nothing can be done without hope and confidence."

- Helen Keller

The final level, Self-Monitoring, is the process of leading in the absence of any formalized structure (Figure 1.11). At this level, sustainability emerges.

Figure 1.11: Level 4 – Self-Monitoring

Write what you learned from the data collected in the implementation of your self-mentoring plan in the space provided on the following page after the previous example.

Taylor's Self-Mentoring Plan

I realize that I cannot change the people that I work with so it is inherent on me to change how I react to these individuals. My data tells me that I allow people to frustrate me too many times and for too long of a period of time. I have employed some tips to deal with difficult people. I tried two of the tips and the data suggests I reduced my distraction time. I decreased my level of frustration and over the span of several weeks, I noticed that these individuals are less of a distraction to me. I am going to try some other techniques over time but for now, I have some safeguards in place. It's working!

Write an overview of your data in the following space.

YOUR Self-Mentoring Plan

Sustainability

While leadership is often viewed as key to *sustainability* (Fullan, 2001; Datnow & Stringfield, 2000), *commitment* is equally important. Oakes, Quartz, Ryan, and Lipton (1999) believed that, unless there is a commitment by those involved, the unwanted behaviors return. Differing from a mentoring or coaching relationship, as a self-mentor, you don't have someone to push you to perfection, so you must determine how to sustain the changes you have made in either your routine or your habits.

There are two methods to assist in sustaining your success. If the new practice is embedded easily into your routine, then you don't need to monitor. If you feel you need to monitor your progress, then develop a monitoring plan. Each expectation is unique and may require a different means to reach the same objective: sustainability.

Jennings developed a plan to monitor the changes he addressed in his plan. The following is Jennings' plan.

Jennings' Self-mentoring Monitoring Plan
I will continue to select projects on a prioritized basis by establishing a deadline to map backwards, incorporating scheduled checkpoints for feedback, reflection, final draft read, and a realistic work schedule with adequate time to complete a quality project. I don't need to monitor my efforts to produce quality projects. I believe I now have a process in place to organize and prioritize my projects. I am going to continue to use self-mentoring in other areas of my personal and professional life, as needed, now that I have a leadership process in place.

Write your monitoring plan in the following space. Be specific in your monitoring efforts.

Self-Mentoring Monitoring Plan

Once you have finalized your monitoring plan, you have completed self-mentoring. You are now a self-mentor. You join the ranks of many that have learned to take control of their lives. You can begin the process all over again if you have another expectation or enjoy your triumph knowing you can call upon your inner leader when needed. Now your inner leader will not be so dormant and will be visible throughout your future endeavors. *Congratulations!*

Ten Steps in Self-mentoring.

As a reminder, there are ten basic steps in self-mentoring:.

1. Brainstorm expectations.
2. Select ONE expectation.
3. Develop strategies for meeting the expectation.
4. Isolate ONE - TWO strategies for the expectation.
5. Align the strategy(s) with a method of measurement.
6. Establish a timeline for collecting data.
7. Collect data over a period of time.
8. Sort and analyze data.
9. Develop a plan from the data.
10. Monitor the plan.

Begin the process again and again until you reach your desired level of performance or productivity.

Chapter Summary

From this chapter we learned how to develop a monitoring plan in order to sustain or maintain new behaviors or targeted change. Sustainability is key in self-mentoring. Since you don't have others to push you or make sure you are successful, you must develop a method to either embed the practice or continue to monitor progress until such a time as the practice is embedded into your daily or weekly routine. Self-mentoring is a ten-step process that can be repeated with a new expectation when you are ready to change or alter something in your performance or environment. This chapter concludes the final level in self-mentoring.

Self and Peer-Reflection Activities

- Reflect on your work to meet your expectation and the methods used to measure and ascertain your progress.
- Share your success with friends or colleagues.
- Talk to others about the process and think about what changes you would make to it, were you to repeat the process.
- Develop a process to ensure your continued success.
- Write your monitoring plan and share it with colleagues or friends for feedback.

SECTION III

THE APPLICATION OF SELF-MENTORING™

8

The Study of Self-Mentoring

"Confidence is what you have before you understand the
problem."

- *Woody Allen*

It became necessary in the infancy of self-mentoring to conduct
studies to determine if self-mentoring could be beneficial to others
and *HOW* it was beneficial. The studies, for the most part, were
predominantly in educational environments –public school district
teachers and university faculty.

Self-Mentoring Studies

The first study was a pilot in a school district that is now in its
third year of continual data collection. There were less than a dozen
teachers in the first study; all were beginning teachers that
volunteered. Another nearby school district joined during the
second year of the original study and is now in its second year. The
results for each study have been analogous. Teachers continuously

gain confidence and demonstrate increased self-efficacy after participating in self-mentoring.

Self-mentoring was also introduced to higher education faculty at a southeastern university in North Carolina through a call for volunteers by the university's Center for Teaching Excellence (CTE). The faculty members, from the School of Nursing, were not new to the profession but new to the university. While they were accomplished researchers, one faculty member was struggling in the new environment and with the organization at large. Most astonishing to the faculty members, as they explained, was the simplicity of self-mentoring as something they admitted to knowing they should do but never took the time to think about how to put it all together. After being introduced to self-mentoring, each faculty member developed an implementation plan and began the process. The results were consistent with the public school teacher studies.

While additional studies are not being conducted with higher education faculty at this time, self-mentoring is being used at the university level through different departments and by department chair(s) to support newly hired or existing faculty as needed. The Center for Teaching Excellence maintains the service on their webpage for all faculty campus-wide, as needed.

In addition to the educational sectors in the United States, self-mentoring is being introduced to Australian administrators as a support for those leaders who often feel isolated in leadership roles. This study is in the planning stage, so those results are not available at the time of this publication.

In addition to the adult studies in self-mentoring, new research has been focused on students. Self-mentoring is being introduced to high school students to determine if the same results are yielded with young adults. At the time of this publication, the study had just begun so information was not readily available. So, there are additional findings on the horizon that may shed more light on self-mentoring and the impact it has on additional individuals or groups. A detailed overview of the initial studies in the two school districts will be the focus of this chapter.

In The Beginning: A Pilot Study

A rural school district in North Carolina was the focus of the first study. The school district was eager to find support for teachers either in danger of being placed on improvement plans or who were new and lacked experience. The county did have a Beginning Teacher (BT) support program that provided mentors for the first three years of a new teachers' career, so self-mentoring was viewed as a potential option for additional support. It was viewed as an intriguing idea – the thought that mentoring could be internally driven. The impetus for the study was the need to know if and how self-mentoring could be used to strengthen and build leaders and in this case, teacher leaders. The following questions were derived:

- *In what ways does self-mentoring support individual prek-12 teachers classroom instructional practice; and*
- *In what ways will self-mentoring support teachers in leadership roles?*

A grounded theory was applied since this theory supported rich descriptive data often captured in qualitative inquiry such as interviews, which were considered indispensable in data collection. A qualitative method was deemed as most suited to uncovering the unexpected and exploring new domains. The benefit of using grounded theory is that this emergent theory is related to the participants' perceived reality rather than to what the researcher, prior to conducting the research, assumes to be true (Marshall and Rossman, 2010).

Teacher Volunteers

There were nine teachers, one male and eight female, who were selected by the local school district or who volunteered to be participants. The only male participant dropped out for unknown reasons at the beginning of the pilot and is not included in the following demographics. The teacher participants taught in grades 1-3 and 6-12 and prior to the pilot year, taught in grades K-1, 3, and 5-12, which was representational of elementary, middle, and high schools. The average teaching experience for the participants was 4.3 years (3-5 years of experience). The participants were between the ages of 20-30, three were between 31-40 years old and one participant was between 51-60 years old. All participants lived in the county and were natives to the area. None of the participants had acquired education beyond a bachelor's degree. In regard to mentoring experiences, seven of the participants had 3 years of prior mentoring and one participant had four years of mentoring. Each of the teachers involved in the study reportedly were attending due to a need to have a stronger presence in the classroom or school setting as both a teacher and a school leader.

As a qualitative study, interviews were used as the primary data source and data was collected before, during, and after four scheduled seminars during the school year. Additional data was collected from participant's journals, seminar videos, seminar group and individual observations, and pre- and post-seminar questionnaires. Pre-and post-assessments were used to collect data on what each participant knew about self-mentoring, involvement in mentoring programs, and leadership initiatives. These data sources were used to cross-reference with the primary and additional data sources. Without interview or survey materials available on self-mentoring, mentoring survey instruments that had been previously validated and reviewed reliable were used.

Self-Mentoring Seminars

The participants met over a period of nine months in four seminars that were approximately two or more hours in duration. The seminars aligned with the levels in self-mentoring: Seminar 1: Self-Awareness, Seminar 2: Self-Development, Seminar 3: Self-Reflection, and Seminar 4: Self-Monitoring. The teachers were from different schools and while some differences in climate were noted from school to school, it was acknowledged that they were in an overarching supportive culture.

During Level 1 Seminar, the participants completed leadership assessments and developed individual expectations. From the group, two primary expectations emerged: to become a stronger leader in the school environment and/or to become a better teacher in the classroom. At the completion of the first seminar, each teacher signed a self-mentoring contract as a testament of commitment.

During Level 2 Seminar, each teacher articulated an expectation, developed measurable strategies, aligned activities, established a timeline for implementation, and selected appropriate measurement methods to assess and evaluate the progress. Each teacher committed to a set amount of time each week during which they would concentrate on meeting the expectation.

Level 3 Seminar complimented the previous work as the participants reviewed the data they collected, analyzed the information, reflected on the findings, and gathered additional data if needed.

During the Level 4 seminar, the focus was on the continued efforts to self-mentor in the absence of any formalized structure or external support from the researchers. Teachers were provided time to reflect in groups by sharing and reviewing available data. Recommendations for future planning and goal setting occurred and each individual developed a monitoring plan.

Data Collection & Analysis

The primary source of data collection during the study was interviews. During the seminars, other data sources were noted such as observations, videos, journals, photos, reflection notes, small group discussions, email exchange, and written responses. Videotaping was used to document the seminar content and delivery method. Facilitator observations were reviewed following each seminar.

Manual data coding was applied to the open-ended individual and group interviews. The first cycle coding was In Vivo and a second cycle utilized pattern coding (Saldana, 2009). Additional analytical data was collected from observations, journal entries, teacher interactions, and related documents. This data was cross-referenced with the interview results. During the first cycle coding, two categories emerged from the teacher interviews: instructional and teacher leadership. In both of these categories, there were classroom (interior) and school-wide (exterior) indicators. Confidence emerged as the most prominent theme and self-efficacy was secondary as noted in Table 1.2. Second cycle coding yielded similar patterns during data comparison and supported initial reviews.

Table 1.2: Self-Mentoring Constructs

	Interior (Classroom)	Exterior (Outside Classroom)
Confidence	Increased (Decision-making, risk taking, leadership)	Increased (Volunteerism, chairing meetings, problem-solving, PLC organizer, Leadership roles)
Self-efficacy	Increased (Classroom activities, awareness, instructional practices)	Increased (Public speaking during groups and in formal settings)

Findings

The results suggested the teachers participating in this study gained confidence as instructional leaders in the classroom and teacher leaders in the school-wide environment.

Instructional Leadership

The teachers reported feeling more confident in classroom management. They were more inclined to assist other teachers and share ideas. "I was more comfortable in my subject area – always comfortable but now more comfortable," shared a teacher. Another teacher, in reply to a question about how instructional practice was improved, explained, "During a Math lesson, I realized sooner that manipulates needed to be supplied."

Teacher Leadership

The teachers all shared that they were empowered to make decisions and determine methods to meet their expectation. As teachers began working through strategies, an elementary teacher who struggled with assuming a school-wide leadership role as chair of a professional learning community (PLC) team meeting excitedly typed the following, in an email exchange, between seminars:

> I made a decision about our PLC at [school]. Three of the four ED teachers can meet together. Number 4 cannot because of students, lunch, or homebound responsibilities. So, I decided to meet with the majority. The last meeting was in Number 4's room because she could not leave her students. So, we met in there.

District officials, who were not a part of the study but asked to be present during all the seminars, reported observable increased confidence in participants during the program. A memo sent by an observing school official to the district superintendent read, "*The self-mentoring session … was exceptionally powerful. [I] am pleased with how productive this session was. The participants stated this was one of the best Professional Development sessions that they have ever been a part of."* The teachers reported the control over their own achievements from personal endeavor was empowering. They believed this sense of accomplishment was motivational and would be sustainable. With the knowledge of how to self-mentor and meet expectations, each teacher perceived sustainability would become a norm of operation.

Self and peer reflections were acknowledged as the most effective tool in self-mentoring by the majority of teachers in all studies. "Reflection makes you more aware of what you are doing so you can correct it," explained one teacher. "Reflection provided confidence to be able to support other colleagues," shared another teacher, " And I believe I will continue to gain confidence as a leader."

An interesting revelation resulted in the final review of the system evaluation pre and post questionnaire data. The teachers were more critical of the leadership of their organization and ranked it lower after completing self-mentoring seminars than prior to the training. Assumptions were drawn that, as the teachers became more confident in leadership roles, they became more critical of the organization.

Conclusions

While the first study revealed interesting revelations, each additional study began to build on the same foundational basis. Self-mentoring served to increase the confidence in the participating individuals as well as heighten self-efficacy as leaders.

A study involving another school district located in North Carolina highlights a two-week self-mentoring student engagement strategy that was implemented by a teacher. Frustrated with student performance, the teacher implemented engagement activities to determine if student writing performances would improve. She identified new strategies to include in her instruction, implementing each engagement activity for two weeks to collect student writing samples in comparison. The photos in Illustration 1.3 and 1.4 on the following page exhibit pre and post student's writing. The student work sample on the left hand side is prior to the teacher implementing her engagement strategy. The student work sample to the right is after the teacher altered some activities in the classroom. Students were able to write more detailed description when assigned a classroom writing assignment. You can see a significant difference in the student's writing sample.

Results can be startling when you actually collect data and take the time to analyze it. As the teachers began to understand the power they had to make a difference through simple changes in their own behavior or habits, their confidence increased. As their confidence was boosted, their self-efficacy also increased.

Illustration 1.3: Writing Sample A

Illustration 1.4: Writing Sample B

The studies suggest, and as evidenced in the personal testimony, that self-mentors feel a sense of accomplishment, empowerment, and increased confidence in their ability to make change when necessary. If we think of professional effectiveness as encompassing the development of confidence, clarity, and competence (Fullan, 2001), we could assume that self-mentors become professionally effective. This type of effectiveness relates to individual performance. Improved performance can be linked to career advancement.

Chapter Summary

From this chapter, we learned that multiple studies have been conducted on self-mentoring in both public and higher education. The studies yielded similar results. Self-mentoring increases self-confidence and self-efficacy. It provides a path for leaders to emerge through increased confidence in their ability to lead. As individuals gain confidence, their perceived ability to lead is increased and leaders are born.

Self and Peer-Reflection Activities

- Reflect on the results of the studies in self-mentoring.
- Share the results of a study with a friend and discuss how it relates to you or your profession.
- Think about the results that could be possible in your field.

9

The Impact of Self-Mentoring

"I want to thank my parents for giving me confidence
disproportionate to my looks and abilities,
which is what all parents should do."

- Tina Fey on receiving an Emmy for Best Actress, 2008.

So how do we measure the *impact* and *importance* of self-mentoring? Conducting studies is certainly one way of testing impact. This is only a glimpse into how self-mentoring can influence an individual or serve as a valuable practice in the world with mentoring and coaching. It is often from the actual testimony of those who have learned to self-mentor that we can learn the most. Even though the practice is very individualized, those that learn to self-mentor experience similar gains. They have increased self-assurance in their capabilities and they become more confident in their ability to lead.

We can learn more about the impact and importance of self-mentoring from those in the field that have applied the practice of self-mentoring in their environment or implemented it in their work, either for production or performance enhancement.

After a Level 2 training, a district teacher in a second-year session shared how she began measuring a strategy for her classroom,

> I started charting with my class that had the most behavioral issues and staying on-task. I would chart every time someone got off-task and what we were doing and they were doing to get off-task to see if I could find a pattern for what was happening.

At one point, she explained why she was collecting the data and measuring it with her students: she wanted to make sure that they were involved in the process. This was more rewarding to her than her isolated attempts at collecting information. Another teacher, struggling with not just classroom management but with his grasp of English as a second language, used a camera to collect data during instruction. He filmed from the back of the classroom so that he captured not only his classroom presence but also how the students reacted to his instruction. He was shocked that each time he turned his back to the class to write on the board, his students misbehaved. It did not take long for him to detect that the classroom management issue was not the students' problem but his own lack of instructional experience in speaking before a group of high school students, as he explains,

> With the camera, I learned a lot about having a camera in my classroom because it makes me work harder. Especially because even though this is not my first language and then I had a teacher there looking at me all the time and also it helped me to

*recognize things in the classroom. Also checking the students'
behavior ... we have to fix something. The thing that the
weakness was all the time the camera was judging me. What do
you do right? What do you do wrong? And I say anyway I'll be
ready to fix. I am also learning in English. I am learning the United
States in the classroom. I got reflections—not exactly data—I got
reflections about that.*

Self-mentoring is not always isolated to the one behavior you want
to observe. Often, as many of the self-mentors learned, observing
one behavior caused them to notice another that also needed to
be addressed. It was a chain reaction as a teacher shares,

*I noticed one of the things that I wanted to do was when I started
[to] do more facilitating less lecturing. So I think that initially that
helped with that as it went on like week after week, I would find
some other facet that I needed to work on, like I was reading to
fast or I was moving too much. Or I wasn't calling on enough
students. So I mean it was good to work on what I had in mind but
it was also good to pinpoint areas that I wasn't cognizant of what I
was doing.*

Upon the conclusion of the self-mentoring training, teachers were
free to share their reactions to the training. Every individual that
participated in the self-mentoring training applauded the process
and how it changed the way they react to and within a specific
setting, as well as how they viewed their ability to have power over
their environment. One self-mentor explains,

*I definitely thought that the experience was a good thing. I used
student engagement to judge [the success] based on classroom
management on how that would go. And I found a very positive
relationship and I use that a lot and I still use it and plan on using
it next year and using especially the first day of school will use a
survey to get my students a feel on what they like to do. And that*

definitely helped shape my lesson plans that I never would've thought of before.

Educators in the public school systems were able to use self-mentoring in a way that not only impacted their lives as leaders in the classroom, but also impacted the lives of their students. Bandura (1997) explains that when you increase the self-efficacy of a classroom teacher, you also increase the self-efficacy of the students.

However, it was not only teachers in classrooms and their students that benefited from self-mentoring training. When faculty at a university explored self-mentoring, the practice shifted the focus from others' needs to their own, which are often neglected in institutes of higher learning. She explains,

I think it was the coming together of the feeling of being overwhelmed in a new role, some of the reading that I did that (was) recommended … we are so focused on mentoring other people and I feel I'm decent at it … I have a history of advising students and advising patients, but I really never thought of advising myself. I … looked for mentoring from other people until I realized you know, I think it also came in my personal life at time when because of certain things that were going on I was focusing more on my own needs and setting boundaries and setting limits and focusing on what makes me happy. So it happened to come at a time when I think I really needed it.

Regardless of the ability of the individual, we all need to be able to stop and look at what is happening to us and what we are doing in the name of professionalism. Another higher education faculty self-mentor explains,

I really look [at] the analogy of cognitive behavioral therapy, you know once it is in your head, I think there is a potential slip back … I think I have a tendency to overcommit … [For me,]I like having the excel sheet because there are categories and you can look [at] visually and you can say ok what is missing and I also just set meetings with senior faculty here to prepare for my tenure application for next year, which I hadn't thought of doing. I don't know why. But sitting down and saying ok based on what you see, do you see anything that needs to be strengthened or something that is kind of being overdone that I can pull back on.

All of the self-mentors were able to reflect on the experience and see the value in their efforts, as shared,

For some people it's going to be difficult at first. Because they don't like to necessarily reflect on possible weaknesses. But by really looking at your weaknesses they become your strengths. So I just encourage people to go ahead and try and jump into it headfirst, not be too difficult on yourself because everyone has things they can improve upon.

Often those involved in self-mentoring are able to employ techniques or strategies to improve their performance merely by devoting less time to work and eliminating burnout and evidenced by this testimony from another higher education faculty self-mentor. She explains,

With the self-mentoring it is truly, truly one of those things that help keep that fire burning in the profession and it eliminates burn-out. Because it not only deals with your professional self, but it deals with your personal life. And it really requires you to sit back and reflect and think about what are my practices that I am doing now and can I continue on this path that I'm on if, you know, [I'm] taking papers home and grading. I'm putting in 15 hours or more and I have no social life. The truth of the matter is you can't keep that up. One of the major things that I've gain[ed] from self-mentoring is it requires me to think about the entire professional me, as a teacher. So I'm very thankful for the opportunity.

Regardless of the business or industry, there will always be a need for self-mentoring.

If you recall in Chapter 2, you were asked to rate your confidence as a leader. If you have completed a self-mentoring plan, then circle the number in the scale below. On a 1-10 scale with 10 as the highest, now circle your confidence as a leader.

| 1 | 2 | 3 | 4 | 5 | 6 | 7 | 8 | 9 | 10 |

Compare your response with the earlier scale rating. *Has your level of confidence increased or stayed the same? Why do you believe this occurred?*

While self-mentoring directly benefits the individual and indirectly others, such as students in a classroom, it is also advantageous to the organization in building organizational citizenship. *How does self-mentoring benefit the organization as a whole?*

Organizational Citizenship

Self-mentoring promotes and increases commitment to the organization. Self-mentors must inspire, motivate, and lead themselves. This fosters the growth of organizational members and enhances their commitment by elevating expectations. Self-mentors learn to accept responsibility for change within the system and as independent thinkers; they contribute to the overall health of the organization instead of exhausting its resources. They are empowered and now have a process in which to grow and develop. The organizational learning and effectiveness increases and the culture of the system is strengthened, thus providing the energy necessary to build a positive culture. Every organization must work to build a core of self-mentors capable of creating an environment of trust and independence – and so, the organization's citizenship is born. As the core of commitment and capability widens, the citizenship increases and the organization flourishes.

Chapter Summary

This chapter provides individual testimony from educators, university faculty, and business people about the impact and importance of self-mentoring. While self-mentoring increases the confidence and self-efficacy of individuals, it also has an impact on the organization. As self-mentors, individuals become independent thinkers and are more considerate of the organization's needs. When individuals are invested in the system, they create an organizational citizenship.

Self and Peer-Reflection Activities

- Grade your organizational citizenship – is it high or low?
- Reflect on the book you have just read and decide if you think self-mentoring is the right fit for you? For a friend or colleague?
- If you didn't develop a plan but just read the book, in what instance would you consider developing a plan?
- Is there ever a time that you would need to self-mentor? Now or in the future?
- Share the book with a colleague and see what they think about the book.

Conclusion

Self-mentoring can build a support program that adds value to not only new leaders but also strengthens the existing culture of a system. "Leading is everyone's work and … we grow into those understandings when we engage with others to make sense of our world, reach out to bring new [colleagues] into full membership in the community, commit to shared outcomes and develop our identities as owners, not tenants, of our [organizations]." (Barth, 2001, p. 428)

Self-mentoring is not a cure-all, but it is a practice to promote leaders in any setting. Avil Beckford, (2012) agrees that self-mentoring "puts you in the position of power. You take control of your life and journey on the path that is right for you" (p. 1). It is only through practice and continued study in the area of self-mentoring we will learn the importance of advocating for continued self-mentoring practice.

Bibliography

Alfred, G., & Garvey, B. (2010). *Mentoring Pocketbook.* (2010) Alresford, UK: Management Pocketbooks, Ltd.

Allen, T.D., Eby, L.T., O'Brien, K.E., & Lentz. E. (2008). The state of mentoring research: A qualitative review of current research methods and future research implications. *Journal of Vocational Behavior, 73*(3), 343-357. (p. 24/29) Retrieved from http://0www.sciencedirect.com.uncclc.coast.uncwil.edu/science/article/pii/S000187910700074

Allen, T.D., Eby, L.T., Poteet, M.L., Lentz, E., & Lima, L. (2004). Career benefits associated with mentoring for proteges: A meta-analysis. *Journal of Applied Psychology,* 89(1), 127-136.

Beckford, A. (, 2012, April). Self-Mentoring: An Idea for the Twenty-First Century. http://theinvisiblementor.com/2012/03/26/self-mentoring-an-idea-for-the-twenty-first-century/

Bandura, A. (1997). *Self-efficacy: the exercise of control.* New York: Freeman.

Bandura, A., & Locke, E. (2003). Negative self-efficacy and goal effects revisited. *Journal of Applied Psychology*, 88, 87-99.

Barth, R. S. (2001). Teacher leader. *Phi Delta Kappan 82*(6), 443–49.

Berman, E. M., & West, J. P. (2008). Managing emotional intelligence in U.S. cities: A study of social skills among public managers. *Public Administration Review,* 68(4)742-758.

Bond, N., & Hargreaves, A. (2014). The power of teacher leaders: Their roles, influences, & impact. Kappa Delta Phi in partnership with New York; NY: Routledge, Taylor, & Francis Group.

Burk, H. G., & Eby, L. T. (2010). What keeps people in mentoring relationships when bad things happen? A field study from the protégé's perspective. *Journal of Vocational Behavior,* 77, 437-446. doi: 10.1016/j.jvb.2010.05.011

Caraccioli, L.A. (1760). *'The true mentor, or, an essay on the education of young people in fashion',* J. Coote at the Kings Arms in Paternoster Row, London.

Carden, A. (1990). Mentoring and adult career development, *The Counselling Psychologist, 18*(2), 275-299.

Carr, M. (2011, March 15). The Invisible Teacher: A Self-Mentoring Sustainability Model. Virtual Mentoring Conference. Watson College of Education, Outreach Alliance. UNCW: Wilmington, North Carolina.

Carr, M. (2011). *The Invisible Teacher: A self-mentoring sustainability model.* Wilmington, NC: University of North Carolina Wilmington, Watson College of Education.

Carr, M. (2012). *The invisible leader: A self-mentoring guide for higher education faculty.* Wilmington, NC: University of North Carolina Wilmington, Watson College of Education.

Clawson, J.G. (1996). Mentoring in the information age. *Leadership and Organization Development Journal, 17*(3), 6-15.

Clutterbuck, D., &Lane, G. (2004). *The situational mentor,* Aldershot, UK :Gower Publishing.

Darwin, A (2000). Critical reflections on mentoring in work settings. *Adult Education Quarterly, 50*(3),197-211.

Datnow, A., & Springfield, S. (2000). Working together for reliable school reform. *Journal of Educational for Students Placed at Risk, 5(1 & 2),* 183-204. (p. 85)

Fénélon, F.S. de la M. (1808). *The Adventures of Telemachus,* Vols 1 and 2, trans. Hawkesworth, J., Union Printing Office, St. John's Square, London.

Forbes. (2014). Forbes Magazine. Internet poll (http://www.forbes.com/pictures/mkl45edige/4-university-professor/).

Fullan, M. (2001). *The new meaning of educational change (3rd ed).* New York: Teachers College Press. (p. 85)

Fullan, M. (2008). *The six secrets of change.* San Francisco, CA: John Wiley & Sons.

Garvey, B. (1995). Healthy signs for mentoring. *Education and Training, 37*(5), 12-19.

Garvey, B. (2014). *A very short, slightly interesting and reasonably cheap book on Coaching and Mentoring (2nd ed).* UK: Sage.

Garvey, B., Stokes, P.,&Megginson, D. (2008). *Coaching and mentoring: Theory and practice*. London, UK: Sage Publications.

Hasbrouck, J. (2007). Student focused coaching: A model for reading coaches. *The Reading Teacher, 60*(7) 690-693.

Hesselbein, F., Goldsmith, M., &Beckhard, R. (1997). *The organization of the future*. San Francisco: Jossey Bass Publications.

Honoria. (1793). *The female mentor or select conversations,* Vols 1 & 2. London, The Strand: T. Cadell.

Honoria. (1796). *The female mentor or select conversations*, Vol. 3. London, The Strand: T. Cadell.

Huang, C. A., &Lynch, J. (1995). Mentoring: The TAO of giving and receiving wisdom. New York, NY: HarperCollins Publishers, Inc.

Jung, C.J. (1958). *Psyche and symbol. New York:* Doubleday.

Kram, K.E. (1983). Phases of the mentor relationship. *Academy of Management Journal, 26*(4),608–25.

Kram, K.E., & Chandler, D.E. (2005). Applying an adult development perspective to developmental networks. *Career Development International, 10*(6/7), 548-566.

Lambert, L. (2003). Leadership redefined: An evocative context for teacher leadership. *School Leadership and Management, 23*(4), 421–30.

Lattimore. R. (1965). *The Odyssey of homer. New York: NY:* Harper Perennial

Levinson, D.J., Darrow, C.N., Klein, E.B., Levinson, M.H., & McKee, B. (1978). *The seasons of a man's life*. New York: Knopf.

Lezotte, L. W., &McKee, K. M. (2002). *Assembly required: A continuous school improvement system*. Okemos, MI: Effective Schools Products, Ltd.

Marshall, C., &Roseman, G. B. (2010). *Designing qualitative research (5ᵗʰ ed)*. Thousand Oaks: CA. Sage Publications.

Mcauley, M. J. (2003). Transference, countertransference and mentoring: the ghost in the process, *British Journal of Guidance & Counselling, 31*(1), 11-23.

Mullen, E. (1994). Framing the mentoring relationship as an information exchange. *Human Resource Management Review,* 4(3), 257–281.

Murray, M. (2001). *Beyond the myths and magic of mentoring: How to facilitate an effective mentoring process*. CA: Jossey-Bass.

Nakamura, J., &Shernoff, D. J. (2009). Good mentoring: Fostering excellent practice in higher education. San Francisco; CA: Jossey-Bass Books.

Oakes, J., Quartz, K., Ryan, S., & Lipton, M. (1999). *Becoming good American schools*. San Francisco, CA: Jossey Bass Publications.

Patterson, K., Grenny, J, McMillan, R.,& Switzler, A. (2012). *Crucial conversations: Tools for talking when stakes are high*. McGraw Hill Publishing.

Pixar University. Retrieved from https://www.youtube.com/watch?v=ngvKmKJLyD4

Ragins, B. R. (1989). Barriers to mentoring: the female manager's dilemma, *Human Relations, 42*(1), 1-23.

Ragins, B. R. (1994, April). Gender and mentoring: A research agenda, presented at the 40th annual meeting of the *South Eastern Psychological Association*, New Orleans, LA.

Ragins, B. R., & Cotton, J.L. (1991). Easier said than done: Gender differences in perceived barriers to gaining a mentor. *Academy of Management Journal, 34*(4),939-952

Ragins, B. R., &Scandura, T. A. (1997). The way we were: Gender and the termination of mentoring relationships. *Journal of Applied Psychology, 82*.

Ragins, B. R., Scandura, T.A. (1999). Burden or blessing? Expected costs and benefits of being a mentor, *Journal of Organisational Behavior, 20*(4),493-509.

Rix, M., & Gold, J., (2000). With a little help from my academic friend: Mentoring change agents. *Mentoring and Tutoring, 8*(1), 47-62.

Saldana, J. (2009). *The coding manual for qualitative researcher*. Thousand Oaks, CA: Sage.

Schein, E. H. (1992). *Organizational culture and leadership*. San Francisco, CA: Jossey Bass.

Schoenfeld, A. C., &Magnan, R. (2004). Mentoring in a manual: Climbing the academic ladder to tenure. Madison, WI: Atwood Publishing.

Sheehy, G. (1976). *Passages: Predictable crises of adult life*. New York: E.P. Dotton Inc.

Sheehy, G. (1996). *New passages: Mapping your life across time*. London, UK: Harper Collins.

Thomas, N., & Saslow, S. (2011). Improving productivity through coaching and mentoring. The Institute of Executive Development (editor: clomedia.com)

Whitworth, L, Kimsey-House, H., & Sandahl, P. (1998). *Co-Active coaching: New skills for coaching people toward success in work and life.* Palo Alto; CA: Davies-Black Publishing.

Wren, J. T. (1995). *The leader's companion: Insights on leadership through the ages.* New York: The Free Press.

Zaleznik, A. (1997). Managers and leaders: Are they different? *Harvard Business Review,* May-June pp 67-78.

Zey, M. C. (1984). *The mentor connection: Strategic alliances in corporate life.* Homewood, IL: Dow Jones-Irving, US.

About the Author

Marsha Carr joined the faculty at the Watson College of Education at the University of North Carolina Wilmington after 35 years of service in private and public education. Carr, the first female school superintendent in her district as well as the youngest superintendent, served for over a decade as a superintendent of schools in West Virginia. Prior to this appointment, she served as a Pre-K – 12th grade school principal, a Director of Curriculum & Instructional Technology, and as a reading specialist. While a reading specialist in an inner city school, frustrated by the lack of available reading materials, Carr began to travel and study whole language in Australia and New Zealand educational systems. In 1993, Carr designed a 20-book emergent level reading series named StoryMakers, which became an international success and was later published in two languages.

Carr was named Teacher of the Year in Allegany County, Maryland and was recognized by the Maryland House of Delegates, as well as received the Maryland Governor's Citation for her work. In 1994, Carr was honored with the National Milken Family Educator Award, the most coveted educator award, and joined a prestigious family of outstanding educators around the nation. More recently, Carr was honored as a Fulbright specialist. She has presented at over a hundred conferences and been published in numerous educational magazines and journals. She is the author of Educational Leadership: From Hostile Takeover to a Sustainable –Successful System and a co-author of The School Improvement Planning Handbook: Focusing on Transition to Turnaround.

Carr is owner of Edu-tell, a consulting company that specializes in self-mentoring™, a leadership development program Carr designed and trademarked. She is the author of three self-mentoring manuals: The Invisible Teacher: A self-mentoring sustainability model workshop guide; The Invisible Leader: A self-mentoring sustainability model for higher education faculty; and The Invisible Student: A Self-mentoring Guide for Middle/High School Students.

Carr resides in Wilmington, North Carolina with her husband, Jennings, and their two dogs, Bailey and Phoenix.

Made in the USA
Charleston, SC
22 March 2015